Betty Crocker's COOKING CALENDAR

A Year-Round Guide to Meal Planning with Recipes and Menus

•

Illustrated by
GLORIA KAMEN and ALICE GOLDEN

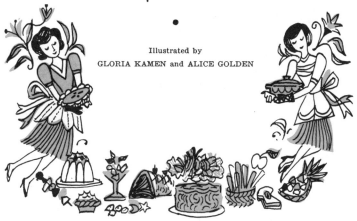

ISBN: 978-0-470-41963-2
Facsimile Edition 2009

Manufactured in China
10 9 8 7 6 5 4 3 2 1

We're excited to bring you this treasured edition of *Betty Crocker's Cooking Calendar*. All the recipes are exactly as they appeared in the original 1962 cookbook. Some ingredients have changed over the years, so you will want to use today's ingredients and methods when making these recipes. Food safety concerns have also changed over the years, so please turn to page 172 for Today's Food Safety information.

WILEY

Dear Friend,

Here is a book that is really two books in one. First of all it is a cook book written to inspire you to lend variety to your meals by using fresh fruits and vegetables when they are at their peak of flavor and are most plentiful.

At the same time it is a calendar book with space to note family birthdays and anniversaries, holidays and appointments—plus famous dates of years gone by and homey mottoes.

You will find a section for each month, with appetizing recipes for featured fruits and vegetables— savory one-dish dinners, flavorful salads, succulent vegetable dishes, glamorous desserts, together with tender meats and fluffy hot breads to round out meals for both every day and entertaining.

We hope you will find this book handy, not only as a source of new and delicious recipes but as a record of family activities.

Sincerely,

Betty Crocker

P. S. You will notice that the recipes in this book specify unsifted flour. Here's all you have to do:

Dip nested dry measuring cups into flour sack or canister.

Level off with spatula or straight-edged knife. (Do not tap cup or pack more flour into cup before leveling off.)

Stir flour with other dry ingredients thoroughly to blend.

····—◄ CONTENTS ►—····

Janus am I: oldest of potentates!
Forward I look and backward and below.
I count—as god of avenues and gates—
The years that through my portals come and go.
—HENRY WADSWORTH LONGFELLOW

Flower: Snowdrop   **Gem:** Garnet

January honors Janus, the Roman god of doorways; hence, the god of beginnings. The early Romans believed that the outcome of every important undertaking depended on the blessing which this god bestowed upon its outset. Janus was always pictured with two faces, one looking to the future and one looking back at the past. And indeed, the month of January does have two faces. It is the time to look back upon the experiences of the past year and try to profit from them in the year ahead. In other words, it is the time for those New Year's resolutions.

During the first week of the new year, make it a practice to get out a handy calendar and jot down the birthdays and wedding anniversaries of your family and friends. It is interesting to note that some people appreciate your remembrance of their anniversary far more than of their birthday. If you plan to give an anniversary gift, make it an appropriate one (see page 68).

My favorite reading on long January evenings is the seed catalogs—armchair gardening begins this month. It is also a good time to go over recipe files. It was on such nights that our great-grandmothers, sitting by the fire, crocheted the bedspreads that are our pride and joy while their daughters (our mothers) pulled taffy, roasted chestnuts, and made sachets. Here are directions for making a delightful orange pomander:

> Stud a thick-skinned, flawless orange with whole cloves, covering the entire surface as thickly as possible. Roll in a mixture of equal parts of orris root (you can get this from your druggist), ground cinnamon, and allspice. Wrap in tissue paper and store in a dark place for four weeks. Shake off surplus powder and tie a pretty ribbon around the orange. Your pomander will emit its nostalgic fragrance for months, even years.

The beginning of the year is a good time to renew the closeness between parents and children—perhaps over a checkerboard or, better yet, with something special. I have a dear friend who encourages the cold-weather custom of assembling her entire family for a pre-bedtime snack consisting of hot drinks (cocoa or mint tea) and coffee cake.

January is also known as the month for white sales. It is a good practice to go over your linen closet the first week in January and make a list of those vanished washcloths, torn tea towels, and shapeless bath mats that need to be replaced. Then go forth into the bargain battle armed with your list, a notation of the exact sizes of sheets that are needed (see page 15), and an awareness of the amount of closet space at home. A bargain is no bargain if there's no room for it, or if it doesn't fit.

JANUARY RED-LETTER FOODS:
BROCCOLI AND ORANGES

TIPS ON BUYING ORANGES
*1 medium orange yields ⅓ to ½ cup juice and
1 to 2 tbsp. rind.*

Signs of Quality:

For slices or sections, buy thick-skinned oranges, light for size; for juice, buy thin-skinned oranges, heavy for size.

Types of Oranges:

Navel (navel formation opposite stem end): Thick, bright orange peel, seedless; usually used for slices or sections.

Valencia: Few seeds, thinner skin; use for both juice and sections.

Plentiful Vegetables	*Other Available Vegetables*	*Plentiful Fruits*
Broccoli	Artichokes	Apples
Brussels Sprouts	Beets (Late)	Avocados
Cabbage	Greens	Bananas
Carrots	Mushrooms	Grapefruit
Cauliflower	Peppers	Lemons
Celery	Rutabagas	Oranges
Eggplant	Sweet Potatoes	Pears (Winter)
Onions (Dry)	and Yams	Tangerines
Parsnips		
Potatoes		
Turnips		
Winter Squashes		

1

"Every day is a fresh beginning."—Susan Coolidge

2

Sprinkle chilled orange slices with confectioners' sugar and coconut.

3

"Light suppers make a long life."—Old English Proverb

4

For Viennese coffee, float whipped cream in each cup.

5

1925—Nellie Ross, first U.S. woman governor, inaugurated in Wyoming.

Twelfth Night is a day of song and gift-giving in many foreign countries. Make it an occasion here, too—perhaps a song-fest with coffee and coffee cake for all the neighbors.

ORANGE STREUSEL COFFEE CAKE

2 cups unsifted Gold Medal Flour
1 tsp. salt
½ cup sugar
2 tsp. baking powder
1 tbsp. grated orange rind
1 egg, slightly beaten
½ cup milk
½ cup orange juice
⅓ cup vegetable oil
Streusel Topping (below)

Grease a 10" pie pan or two 8" round layer pans. Stir flour, salt, sugar, and baking powder together in bowl. Add orange rind. Make a well and add egg, milk, orange juice, and oil. Stir only enough to dampen flour; batter should be lumpy. Turn into prepared pan. Sprinkle with Streusel Topping. Bake 10" cake in 375° oven 35 min.; bake 8" cakes in 400° oven 30 min. Serve in wedges. *6 to 8 servings.*

Streusel Topping: Mix ¼ cup Gold Medal Flour and ½ cup sugar in bowl. Cut in 2 tbsp. butter until consistency of corn meal.

◖◗◖◗◖◗◖◗◖◗◖◗◖◗◖◗◖◗

Weekend Dinner

*Oven-baked Chicken
with Orange Sauce
Buttered Brussels Sprouts
Carrot-Raisin Salad
Hot Biscuits
Chocolate Pudding

◖◗◖◗◖◗◖◗◖◗◖◗◖◗◖◗◖◗

OVEN-BAKED CHICKEN WITH ORANGE SAUCE

1 fryer chicken, cut in pieces
½ cup fresh orange juice (1 large or 2 medium oranges)
1 tsp. salt
1 tsp. dry mustard
1 tsp. paprika
¼ tsp. Tabasco
1 to 3 tbsp. grated orange rind
⅓ cup vegetable oil
1 can (4 oz.) sliced mushrooms
  or ¾ cup sliced fresh mushrooms

Heat oven to 400° (mod. hot). Place chicken skin-side-down in single layer in a shallow baking pan. Mix rest of ingredients (except mushrooms) to make sauce and pour over each piece of chicken, coating well. Bake 45 min., basting occasionally. Turn, sprinkle mushrooms over top, baste again with sauce, and bake 15 min. longer. Remove chicken to hot platter and spoon sauce over top. *4 to 6 servings.*

6

Twelfth Night—the feast of the Three Magi, or Three Kings.

7

1789—First presidential election in the United States.

8

"Not to be eager to buy is income."—Cicero

9

1793—First flight in U.S., by balloonist Jean Pierre Blanchard.

10

Easy appetizer: salami and chive cream cheese "sandwiches."

11

1935—Amelia Earhart flew solo from Honolulu to Oakland, Calif.

12

1932—Hattie W. Caraway of Arkansas, first woman elected to U.S. Senate.

❀❀❀❀❀❀❀❀❀❀❀❀❀

Supper Before the Basketball Game

*Ham-Onion-Broccoli Casserole

Raspberry Gelatin Salad

with Peaches

Favorite Pickles

Lemon-filled Lemon Velvet Cake

❀❀❀❀❀❀❀❀❀❀❀❀❀

BROCCOLI WITH BROILED MAYONNAISE

Quick and easy dress-up for a cooked green vegetable.

Place 4 to 6 servings of cooked broccoli in oven-proof dish that may be used for serving. Beat 1 egg white† until stiff but not dry; fold in 1 cup mayonnaise. Spread mixture over broccoli and broil until delicately browned, about 1 min.

How to Prepare Broccoli: Remove large leaves and ends of tough stalk parts. If thick, make 3 to 4 gashes through each stem so stems will cook as quickly as bud tops. Cook standing upright in 1″ boiling salted water 10 to 15 min.

† *See page 172*

HAM-ONION-BROCCOLI CASSEROLE

1 lb. fresh broccoli, cut up, *or*
  1 pkg. frozen cut-up broccoli
1 cup cubed cooked or baked
  ham
1 cup drained whole onions
  (8-oz. can)
2 cups Medium White Sauce
  (p. 157)
2 tsp. dry or prepared mustard
¼ cup grated Cheddar cheese
1 cup unsifted Gold Medal Flour
1½ tsp. baking powder
½ tsp. salt
2 tbsp. chopped parsley
2½ tbsp. vegetable oil
⅓ cup milk

Heat oven to 425° (hot). Cook broccoli until just slightly tender. Drain. Mix with ham and onions in 1½-qt. baking dish. Make White Sauce. Add mustard and cheese; stir until cheese is melted. Pour over ham-broccoli mixture. Place in oven while making biscuits.

Stir flour, baking powder, salt, and parsley together. Pour oil and milk into measuring cup but don't stir. Pour all at once into flour mixture. Stir only until well blended. Take baking dish from oven. Drop biscuits by tablespoonfuls onto hot mixture in baking dish. Bake 25 to 30 min. *6 servings.*

13

1894—Stephen Foster died with 35¢ to his name in New York City.

14

1873—"Celluloid" registered as trade name.

15

1870—Cartoonist Thomas Nast used donkey as Democratic Party symbol.

16

Mayonnaise made in a blender takes only a minute and tastes so good.

17

1810—Birthday of canning process, by French chef Nicholas Appert.

18

"To err is human, to repent divine; to persist devilish."—Franklin

19

1807—Robert E. Lee born, a legal holiday in most southern states.

WILLIAMSBURG ORANGE CAKE

Up-to-date version of a favorite cake of colonial Virginia. See picture on pp. 142-143.

1⅓ cups unsifted Gold Medal Flour
1 cup sugar
2 tsp. baking powder
½ tsp. salt
⅓ cup soft shortening (part butter)
⅔ cup milk
1 tsp. vanilla
1 egg
½ cup cut-up raisins
⅓ cup chopped walnuts
grated rind of 1 orange

Heat oven to 350° (mod.). Grease and flour a 9″ sq. pan. Stir flour, sugar, baking powder, and salt together in mixer bowl. Add shortening, milk, and vanilla. Beat 2 min., medium speed on mixer, scraping bowl constantly. Add egg, raisins, nuts, and rind. Beat 2 more min., medium speed, scraping bowl frequently. Pour into prepared pan. Bake 35 to 40 min. Frost with Orange Icing Royale (below). *12 to 16 servings.*

Orange Icing Royale: Combine 2½ cups sifted confectioners' sugar and ¼ cup soft butter. Blend in 1 tbsp. orange juice and 1 tsp. to 1 tbsp. sherry flavoring until smooth. Spread on cooled cake.

PIN MONEY— How It Started

In the 14th century, pinmakers were allowed to sell their wares only on January 1 and 2. In those days few women had independent incomes, so husbands had to provide money for their annual pin purchases—hence "pin money." On New Year's Day, then, it's proper to get pin money from your husband.

How to Make Orange Shells

Choose perfect oranges. Score orange around middle with knife point; peel skin away from fruit with spoon handle. Make notched edge with kitchen shears.

For an attractive appetizer or salad, fill orange shells with mixed fruits and garnish with mint leaves. For a pretty dessert, fill with fruit sherbet and garnish with orange sections.

20

To freshen French bread, sprinkle with water and heat in hot oven.

21

1907—Carrie Nation raided a Wichita saloon with a hatchet.

22

1901—Queen Victoria died, ending an era and a reign of 64 years.

23

For ease in cutting raisins and dates, use kitchen shears.

24

1848—Gold discovered in California by James W. Marshall.

25

1890—Reporter Nelly Bly circled the globe alone in 72 days.

26

1831—Mary Mapes Dodge, author of "Hans Brinker," born.

⟨o⟩⟨o⟩⟨o⟩⟨o⟩⟨o⟩⟨o⟩⟨o⟩⟨o⟩⟨o⟩⟨o⟩

Ladies' Luncheon

*Turkey Divan

Celery Curls, Radish Roses,

Pickle Fans

Hot Sesame Seed Rolls

*Orange Baked Alaskas

⟨o⟩⟨o⟩⟨o⟩⟨o⟩⟨o⟩⟨o⟩⟨o⟩⟨o⟩⟨o⟩⟨o⟩

TURKEY DIVAN

1½ lb. fresh broccoli *or*
  2 pkg. (10 oz. each) frozen
  broccoli spears
6 slices turkey (about ¼" thick)
  or 1½ to 2 cups pieces of
  turkey
6 slices cheese
1 can (14½ oz.) evaporated milk
1 can (10½ oz.) mushroom soup
1 can (3½ oz.) French fried
  onion rings

Heat oven to 350° (mod.). Cook broccoli to crisp-tender stage. Put turkey in bottom of oblong baking dish, 11½ x 7½ x 1½". Cover with broccoli; top with cheese slices and cover with mixture of milk and soup. Bake 25 min. Cover with onion rings and bake 5 min. more. *4 to 6 servings.*

ORANGE BAKED ALASKAS

See picture on p. 33.

Ahead of time: Shape 6 vanilla ice cream balls. Freeze until solid, 5 to 6 hr. or overnight.

Make orange cups by cutting 3 large seedless oranges in half. Remove fruit and surrounding membrane. Section fruit, removing membrane. Line bottom of orange cups with all or part of orange sections. Chill.

At serving time: Heat oven to 500° (very hot). Make 3-Egg White Meringue (below). Place orange cups on baking sheet and fill with ice cream balls. Quickly cover ice cream with meringue, being careful to seal meringue to edge of cups. Bake 2 to 3 min., or until meringue is slightly browned. Serve immediately. *6 servings.*

Grapefruit Baked Alaskas: Substitute 3 medium-sized grapefruit for oranges.

3-Egg White Meringue: Beat 3 egg whites† with ¼ tsp. cream of tartar until frothy. Gradually beat in 6 tbsp. sugar, a little at a time. Continue beating until stiff.

† *See page 172*

27

Appe-teaser: chilled broccoli buds and carrot sticks with a dip.

∽∾∽∾∽∾∽∾∽∾∽∾∽∾∽∾∽∾∽∾∽∾∽∾∽∾∽∾

28

"Man has his will, but woman has her way."—Oliver Wendell Holmes

∽∾∽∾∽∾∽∾∽∾∽∾∽∾∽∾∽∾∽∾∽∾∽∾∽∾∽∾

29

"I'll be with you in the squeezing of a lemon."—Old Colonial Saying

∽∾∽∾∽∾∽∾∽∾∽∾∽∾∽∾∽∾∽∾∽∾∽∾∽∾∽∾

30

"Home is where the heart is."—Elbert Hubbard

∽∾∽∾∽∾∽∾∽∾∽∾∽∾∽∾∽∾∽∾∽∾∽∾∽∾∽∾

31

1836—America's most famous needlewoman, Betsy Ross, died.

When Headed for a White Sale—

Remember the dimensions of sheets needed for various bed sizes:
TWIN (36"–48" wide) and THREE-QUARTER BEDS (48"–54" wide)—
both need sheets 72" by 108".

DOUBLE BEDS (54"–59" wide)—need sheets 72"–81" by 108".

QUEEN-SIZE BEDS (60" wide)—need sheets 90" by 108".

KING-SIZE BEDS (72" wide by 84" long)—need sheets 108" by 122½".

For extra-long wear, buy muslin with 140 threads to the inch. For
smoothness, buy percales—a popular thread-count is 180 to the inch.

FEBRUARY

It is pleasant to think, just under the snow,
That stretches so bleak and blank and cold,
Are beauty and warmth that we cannot know,
Green fields and leaves and blossoms of gold.
—HEMSTEAD

Flower: Violet or Primrose **Gem:** Amethyst

February is a kind of Johnny-come-lately as months go, for it was the last month added to the old Roman calendar. Named after the *Februa,* the Roman feast of purification which was celebrated at this time, February is the month that gets the extra day in Leap Year. As the last month of the Roman year, one day was added to it every fourth year to compensate for the one-fourth extra day in each year. Years whose dates are divisible by four are Leap Years, with the exception of the century years. Only every four-hundredth century year is a Leap Year; thus, February, 2000, will have the extra day, while February, 2100, will not.

Let's make February tidy-up month. It's a good time to straighten out closets and drawers and to weed out books. Remember that what is one person's trash may be another's treasure. Churches and charitable organizations are often able to make use of an outgrown dress or the yard goods you've never had time to make up. And your local hospital will welcome your once-read paperback books, which will probably yellow and turn brittle if you put them away on a bookshelf. Make it a point, too, to climb up and look at the topmost shelf of your closet. That silver bonbon dish or filigree vase you haven't used in years will probably make someone else happy at a church bazaar.

Although it is still a month of wintry cold, you can bring a breath of spring to February. As soon as forsythia, magnolia, or flowering quince buds begin to swell, bring the cut branches inside for forcing. Stand them in a deep vase with plenty of water at room temperature, perhaps near the register. It will take about ten days for the stalks to blossom out.

Valentine parties are expected in February, but why not try something different—a Mardi Gras party, perhaps, on Shrove Tuesday. And in the real Shrove Tuesday tradition, refreshments should be sausage links and pancakes or waffles topped with maple butter (a combination of 1 cup maple syrup for each ½ cup butter, beaten until fluffy). In addition to using griddles on every unit of your range, borrow some additional electric units or frypans and line them right up on the buffet table. Have the batter ready in huge pitchers, and cook while your guests look—some of them may even want to flip their own.

SHROVE TUESDAY, 1620

"*. . . there is a bell rung call'd the Pancake-Bell, then there is a thing call'd wheaten floure which cookes do mingle with water, eggs, spice and other tragicall, magicall enchantments into the form of a Flip-Jack, call'd Pancake, which ominous incantation the people do devour very greedillie.*" —JOHN TAYLOR, the Water Poet

FEBRUARY RED-LETTER FOODS:
CABBAGE AND BANANAS

Plentiful Vegetables	Other Available Vegetables	Plentiful Fruits
Beets (Late)	Artichokes	Apples
Cabbage	Broccoli	Avocados
Carrots	Brussels Sprouts	Bananas
Cauliflower	Celery Root	Grapefruit
Celery	Greens	Oranges (Navel)
Eggplant	Parsnips	Tangerines
Mushrooms	Peppers	
Onions (Dry)	Rutabagas	
Potatoes	Sweet Potatoes	
Turnips	and Yams	
Winter Squashes		

CABBAGE BUYER'S GUIDE
1 lb. serves 3 to 4; makes 4 cups, shredded.
Weight of heads varies from 2 to 5 lb.

Types of Cabbage:

Domestic: Round or flat, slightly compact head; matures late.

Chinese: Cylindrical shape; long, thick light-green leaves.

Red: Red or purple color; strong flavor; solid head.

Signs of Quality:

Head well trimmed, heavy for size; no discolorations or worm holes. Looks fresh, not coarse or puffy.

1

"A snow year, a rich year."—George Herbert

2

Six more winter weeks in store, if sunrays strike the ground hog's door.

3

"Cabbage, like a good wife, is often taken for granted."—Old Saying

4

"To have friends, be one."—Elbert Hubbard

5

To make rice whiter, add 2 tsp. lemon juice to boiling water.

6

"Bread and cheese make a healthy man."—Old French Proverb

7

"God loveth not the speaking ill of anyone in public."—The Koran

✦✧✦✧✦✧✦✧✦✧✦✧✦✧✦✧

Hardy Sailor's Fare

*New England Boiled Dinner

Pickles and Tomato Relish

Tossed Green Salad

Buttermilk Bread (p. 40)

with Strawberry Preserves

Boston Cream Pie

✦✧✦✧✦✧✦✧✦✧✦✧✦✧✦✧

NEW ENGLAND BOILED DINNER

See picture on pp. 34-35.

**3 to 4-lb. corned brisket of beef
8 small onions
8 whole carrots
4 potatoes, halved or quartered
2 turnips, cubed (if desired)
1 green cabbage, cut in wedges**

Place beef in heavy kettle. Cover with hot water. Cover tightly and simmer 3½ to 4 hr., until tender. About 35 min. before meat is done, skim off excess fat and add onions, carrots, potatoes, and turnips. Cover and cook 20 min. Add cabbage and cook another 10 to 15 min. *8 servings.*

CABBAGE AND FRANK JUBILEE

**8 cups coarsely shredded
   cabbage
2 cups Medium White Sauce
   (p. 157)
2 tbsp. prepared mustard
1 lb. wieners, cut diagonally
   in 1½" pieces
1 cup grated Cheddar cheese
2 tbsp. fine bread crumbs**

Heat oven to 350° (mod.). Cook cabbage covered in ½ to 1" boiling salted water, 5 min.; drain. Prepare White Sauce. Add mustard and mix thoroughly. Place half the cabbage in bottom of greased 2-qt. baking dish. Arrange half the wiener pieces on top of cabbage. Pour over half of mustard sauce. Repeat layers. Top with cheese and fine bread crumbs. Cover and bake 35 to 40 min. *5 to 6 servings.*

✦✧✦✧✦✧✦✧✦✧✦✧✦✧✦✧

Pennywise Supper

*Cabbage and Frank Jubilee

Whole Wheat Brown 'N Serve Rolls

Gingerbread with Hot Applesauce

✦✧✦✧✦✧✦✧✦✧✦✧✦✧✦✧

8

"Tell me what you eat, I will tell you what you are."—Brillat-Savarin

9

Top long banana slices with salad dressing and chopped peanuts.

10

"Variety is the best culinary spice."—Gulf City Cook-Book, 1886

11

Blend avocado, tomato, a bit of onion, and Tabasco for a tasty dip.

12

Lincoln's Birthday—a holiday in most states.

13

"Be to her Virtues very kind, be to her Faults a little blind."—Prior

14

St. Valentine's Day—"All mankind loves a lover."—Emerson

◊⟩◊⟩◊⟩◊⟩◊⟩◊⟩◊⟩◊⟩◊⟩◊⟩◊⟩◊⟩

Quick Supper

Hamburger Patties

Pan-fried Potatoes

Peas in Cream

*Banana Roll-ups with Lemon Sauce

◊⟩◊⟩◊⟩◊⟩◊⟩◊⟩◊⟩◊⟩◊⟩◊⟩◊⟩◊⟩

BANANA ROLL-UPS

**1 stick Betty Crocker Pie Crust
  Mix
2 large bananas
¼ cup sugar
¼ tsp. cinnamon
Lemon Sauce (below)**

Heat oven to 450° (hot). Prepare pastry. Roll thin, into a square shape. Cut pastry into 4 pieces. Cut bananas in half crosswise; roll in mixture of sugar and cinnamon. Place each piece of banana on a square of pastry. From each end, fold the pastry in towards the center. Roll lengthwise to cover banana; place on ungreased baking sheet. Sprinkle with remaining cinnamon and sugar. Bake 12 min., or until golden brown. Serve with Lemon Sauce. *4 servings.*

Lemon Sauce: Combine ½ cup butter, 1 cup sugar, ¼ cup water, 1 egg, well beaten, 3 tbsp. lemon juice, and grated rind of 1 lemon in saucepan. Cook, stirring constantly, just until mixture comes to a boil. *Makes 1⅓ cups.*

BANANA CHIFFON PIE

Just the dessert for your next bridge party.

**9″ Baked Pie Shell
1 envelope unflavored gelatin
  (1 tbsp.)
2 tbsp. cold water
⅔ cup sugar
1 cup mashed ripe banana
  (2 or 3)
¼ tsp. salt
½ to ¾ tsp. nutmeg
3-Egg White Meringue (p. 14)[†]
½ cup whipping cream, whipped**

Dissolve gelatin in cold water. Blend sugar, banana, and salt in saucepan. Place over medium to low heat for about 5 min. Remove from heat and stir in gelatin and nutmeg. Cool until mixture mounds slightly when dropped from a spoon. Fold into meringue. Carefully blend in whipped cream. Pour into cooled baked pie shell and refrigerate until set. Garnish with whipped cream and banana slices (dipped in lemon juice to prevent discoloration).

† *See page 172*

15

1820—Susan B. Anthony was born in South Adams, Mass.

16

"The quarrels of lovers are the renewal of love."—Terence

17

Cream whips more easily when beater and bowl are chilled.

18

1930—Pluto, the ninth planet, discovered at Lowell Observatory, Ariz.

19

1878—Phonograph patented by Thomas Edison.

20

Sprinkle lemon juice on cut apples, bananas, and avocados.

21

"Of all the animals, the boy is the most unmanageable."—Plato

*I prithee send me back my
   heart
Since I cannot have thine;
For if from yours you will not
   part,
Why then shouldst thou have
   mine?*

—SIR JOHN SUCKLING

CHERRY CROWN FROSTING

This frosting, on a white layer cake, will please the family on George Washington's Birthday.

Make Betty Crocker Cherry Fluff Frosting Mix as directed on pkg; reserve ½ cup frosting. Frost between layers and on top and sides. Tint reserved frosting a deeper pink with red food coloring. Complete cake with a deep pink crown around top edge.

CREME VANILLE HEART

½ cup sugar
1 envelope unflavored gelatin
   (1 tbsp.)
¼ tsp. salt
2¼ cups milk
4 egg yolks, slightly beaten†
1 cup cooked rice
1 cup whipping cream,
   whipped stiff
¾ cup mixed candied fruit *or*
   drained crushed pineapple
1 tsp. vanilla

Blend sugar, gelatin, and salt thoroughly in saucepan. Gradually stir in milk and egg yolks. Cook over medium heat, stirring constantly, just until mixture comes to a boil. (Do not boil, or mixture will curdle.) Immediately place pan in cold water; cool until mixture mounds slightly when dropped from a spoon. Fold in remaining ingredients. Pour into a buttered 1-qt. heart-shaped mold or 8 individual heart-shaped molds. Chill until firm, about 4 hr. Unmold and garnish with more whipped cream and maraschino cherries. *8 servings.*

† *See page 172*

22

George Washington's Birthday—a national holiday since 1796.

23

1787—Emma Willard, famous women's educator, born in Berlin, Conn.

24

"Our life is frittered away in detail . . . Simplify, Simplify."—Thoreau

25

Quick snack: beat together 1 cup cold milk and 1 banana, mashed.

26

Let your imagination run riot when topping Shrove Tuesday pancakes.

27

"Whatever you have, spend less."—Samuel Johnson

1879—In Utica, N.Y., Woolworth added up first week's sales of his "5 & 10."

28/29

Happy, Happy, Happy, Happy Birthday to all Leap Year babies!

. . . Daffodils,
That come before the swallow dares, and take
The winds of March with beauty.
—WILLIAM SHAKESPEARE

Flower: Daffodil   **Gem:** Aquamarine

A world anew, fresh and sparkling and full of hope—that is the meaning of spring and of its birth-month, March. With the strength of Mars, the Roman god of war in whose honor this month was named, March sweeps in on the wings of a rushing wind, bringing a renewed joy of living, a tingle of excitement as old as the earth itself. Anything and everything seems possible this month, for it is the beginning of so many things—a new flower season, a new fashion season, and a new housekeeping season.

It is a good time to give your surroundings a first-class reappraisal. On the first sunny day go over your house as your best enemy would. Your impartial inspection may reveal shabby upholstery that you've become used to, woodwork in need of a fresh coat of paint, or wallpaper that is past all ministrations of a light washing. Get out that collection of decorating ideas clipped from your favorite household magazines, and see whether you can apply any of them to your own home. But plan carefully before ripping up, tearing down, or stripping off.

After you have taken a good look at *your* surroundings, go out to the front walk in the bright sunlight and take a critical look at your home's surroundings. Your crocuses, spring snowflakes, and the many varieties of daffodils should now be bobbing their heads. If your garden doesn't boast a bulb display to announce to all that you welcome the arrival of spring, note this month where they could go—in clumps beside the driveway or around the edges of budding deciduous shrubs—and dedicate one afternoon next fall to bulb planting. As for the rest of your yard, is it all that it could be, or does it just get by? A little bit of attention now, in March, will go a long way toward making your total surroundings express the true you later in the year.

The stormy March is come at last,
With wind, and cloud, and changing skies;
I hear the rushing of the blast,
That through the snowy valley flies.

Ah, passing few are they who speak,
Wild, stormy month! in praise of thee;
Yet though thy winds are loud and bleak,
Thou art a welcome month to me.

For thou, to northern lands, again
The glad and glorious sun dost bring,
And thou hast joined the gentle train
And wear'st the gentle name of Spring.

—WILLIAM CULLEN BRYANT

MARCH RED-LETTER FOODS:
ONIONS, LEMONS, AND GRAPEFRUIT

Plentiful Vegetables

Beets (Late)
Cabbage
Carrots
Celery
Greens
Mushrooms
Onions (Dry)
Potatoes (New
and Mature)
Turnips
Winter Squashes

Other Available Vegetables

Artichokes
Broccoli
Brussels Sprouts
Celery Root
Eggplant
Parsnips
Peas
Peppers
Rutabagas
Sweet Potatoes
and Yams

Plentiful Fruits

Apples
Grapefruit
Lemons
Oranges
Pineapples

HINTS ON BUYING ONIONS
1 lb. white onions serves 3 to 4.
Select onions with hard bulbs, thin necks, and dry crackled skin.

Types of Dry Onions:

American: Red, yellow, or white; strong flavor, medium size, globe shape.

Bermuda: White or yellow; mild flavor, flat type.

Spanish or Valencia: White or yellow-brown; mild, sweet, largest in size, globe shape.

Buy for a Purpose:

For vegetable: American or Bermuda, 1 to 2″ in diameter.

For seasoning: Yellow and red.

Other Onion Varieties:

Chives: Slender, tubular, dark-green leaves.

Garlic: Small bulb made up of cloves, white skin.

Shallot: Looks like garlic, but milder, brown skin.

Green onions: Immature bulbs.

Leeks: Larger than scallions, rounded base, solid, flat leaves.

Scallions: Small bulb, thick neck.

1

"Lion-like March cometh in, hoarse with tempestuous breath."—Howells

2

1799—The General Post Office was established by Congress.

3

"Conscience is a mother-in-law whose visit never ends."—H. L. Mencken

4

1933—Frances Perkins, as Labor Secretary, became first woman in Cabinet.

5

"If fruits had mouths they would eat themselves."—Caucasus Proverb

6

"Promise is most given when the least is said."—George Chapman

7

Peel onions under running water to prevent those "onion" tears.

Continental Luncheon

*Onion Pie Elegante

Spinach and Lettuce Salad

Tiny Biscuits

Green Mint Ice Cream

with Pineapple Kabobs (p. 82)

ONION PIE ELEGANTE

Butter Pastry (below, right)
8 slices bacon
2 cups coarsely chopped onions
3 eggs
1 cup commercial sour cream
1¼ tsp. salt
⅛ tsp. pepper
1½ tsp. chopped chives

Heat oven to 475° (very hot). Prepare pastry, roll out and line 9" pie pan. Flute edges; prick with fork. Bake 8 to 10 min.

Reduce oven temperature to 300° (slow). Fry bacon until crisp; crumble. Sauté onions in 2 tbsp. bacon fat until tender. In bowl, beat eggs slightly; stir in sour cream, salt, pepper, chives, onion, and bacon. Pour into baked pie shell. Bake 40 to 50 min., or until silver knife inserted 1" from edge comes out clean. *5 to 7 servings.*

TINY WHOLE GLAZED ONIONS

A festive treatment for onions.

Cook 12 tiny fresh or canned onions with a whole clove in each end. Drain. In skillet, sauté onions gently in ¼ cup butter. Sprinkle with ½ cup brown sugar. Turn often; cook until golden brown and caramelized. *4 servings.*

FRIED LIVER AND ONIONS

This is the way men like onions—smothering tender slices of liver.

Peel and slice medium sweet onions. Cook in hot bacon fat until golden. Cover and cook slowly until tender. Season with salt and pepper. Remove to warm plate and keep warm while frying liver.

Dip ½" thick slices of calves or baby beef liver (allow ¼ lb. per serving) in flour. Brown in hot fat. Season. Cook over low heat 10 to 15 min., turning once. Serve hot, topped with onions.

Butter Pastry: Stir 1¼ cups unsifted Gold Medal Flour and ¾ tsp. salt together in bowl. Cut in ¼ cup each of butter and soft shortening. Sprinkle on 2½ tbsp. milk, stirring until all flour is moistened. Gather into a ball.

8

"After the snow, the emerald leaves."—George Cooper

● ●

9

1451—Amerigo Vespucci, "Godfather" of America, born.

● ●

10

1852—"Uncle Tom's Cabin " published.

● ●

11

1847—"Johnny Appleseed," John Chapman, died near Ft. Wayne, Ind.

● ●

12

1912—Girl Scouts founded by Juliette Low in Savannah, Ga.

● ●

13

"Appetite, a universal wolf."—Shakespeare

● ●

14

Thinly sliced red onions are delicious and colorful in salads.

◆◇◆◇◆◇◆◇◆◇◆◇◆◇◆◇◆◇

Dining Deliciously

Broiled Ham Slice
with Raisin Sauce

Stuffed Baked Potatoes

Buttered Green Limas

Cottage Cheese Salad

*Lemon Schaum Torte

◇◆◇◆◇◆◇◆◇◆◇◆◇◆◇◆◇◆

GRAPEFRUIT SALADS

Arrange the fruit combinations on salad greens. Garnish gaily with sprigs of water cress or fresh anise. Serve with fruit dressings.

Grapefruit-Pomegranate Salad: Arrange grapefruit sections in petal fashion. Sprinkle with pomegranate seeds.

Grapefruit-Avocado-Persimmon Salad: Alternate slices of avocado and persimmon with sections of grapefruit. Garnish.

Tomato-Grapefruit Salad: Place Tomato Flower Cups (below) on lettuce leaves. Arrange sections of grapefruit and slices of orange around each tomato. Dot with a bit of mayonnaise.

Tomato Flower Cups: Cut tomatoes almost through into 6 sections so they will be open like flowers.

LEMON SCHAUM TORTE
(Angel Pie)

Make Meringue Torte (below). Spread with cooled Lemon Torte Filling (below). Top with 1 cup whipping cream, stiffly whipped. Chill about 12 hr. before serving. *8 to 10 servings.*

Meringue Torte: Heat oven to 275° (slow). Beat 4 egg whites[†] (½ cup) and ¼ tsp. cream of tartar until frothy. Gradually beat in 1 cup sugar, a little at a time. Beat until very stiff and glossy. Tint, if desired, with food coloring. Spread on heavy brown paper on baking sheet in 8 or 9" round. Shape with back of spoon. Bake 60 min. Turn off oven and leave in until cool.

Lemon Torte Filling: Beat 4 egg yolks[†] in small mixer bowl until thick and lemon-colored. Gradually beat in ½ cup sugar. Blend in ¼ cup lemon juice and 2 tbsp. grated lemon rind. Cook over hot water, stirring constantly, until thick, 5 to 8 min. Cool.

† *See page 172*

Winter

✪➤✪➤✪➤✪➤✪➤✪➤✪➤✪➤✪➤✪➤✪➤

Candlelight Supper

*Crown Roast of Pork

*Mushroom Stuffing

Buttered Brussels Sprouts

Tiny Whole Glazed Onions (p. 30)

Grapefruit-Pomegranate Salad (p. 32)

Biscuits, Butter, Honey

Chocolate Chiffon Tarts

✪➤✪➤✪➤✪➤✪➤✪➤✪➤✪➤✪➤✪➤✪➤

CROWN ROAST OF PORK

See picture on p. 36.

Have crown made at meat market from 2 strips of pork loin, containing about 20 ribs (6 to 8 lb.). (For easy carving, have backbone removed.) Season with salt and pepper. Place in roasting pan, bone ends up; wrap bone ends in aluminum foil to prevent excessive browning. Roast uncovered in slow oven (325°) 20 to 25 min. per lb. of meat, 2½ to 3½ hr. An hour before meat is done fill center with 2 qt. Mushroom Stuffing (right). To serve: replace foil wraps on bone ends with crabapples or paper frills. Surround with Brussels sprouts and tiny whole glazed onions. Slice between ribs. *About 12 servings.*

MUSHROOM STUFFING

⅔ cup butter
½ cup finely minced onion
8 cups (2 qt.) coarse or fine bread crumbs or cubes
1 cup chopped celery
2 tsp. salt
½ tsp. pepper
2 tsp. dried sage, thyme, or marjoram
poultry seasoning (to taste)
1 can (6 or 8 oz.) sliced mushrooms *or* 1 lb. fresh mushrooms, sliced.

Melt butter in large heavy skillet. Add onion; cook until yellow. Stir in some of bread crumbs; heat, stirring to prevent excessive browning. Turn into deep bowl. Mix in remaining bread crumbs and other ingredients. For dry stuffing, add little or no liquid. For moist, mix in lightly just enough hot water or broth to moisten dry crumbs. Cool; place in middle of crown roast. Bake. *2 qt.* Garnish with sliced canned water chestnuts.

There is no flavour comparable, I will contend, to that of the crisp, tawny, well-watched, not over-roasted, *crackling* (pig). . . .

. . . wouldst thou have had this innocent grow up to the grossness and indocility which too often accompany maturer swinehood? —CHARLES LAMB
from *A Dissertation upon Roast Pig*

Artichokes were known in Egypt 2,000 years ago, but Egyptians ate what we do not —the stalks and outer leaves. They were popular in Italy in the 15th century, and were introduced to America early in the 20th century by our Italian immigrants in the Central California valley.

STEAMED ARTICHOKES

Plan on 1 French or globe artichoke per person. Cut off 1″ of top with sharp knife. Trim stems leaving ½″ stub. Remove lower leaves and thorny leaf tips. Tie leaves to keep shape. Cook covered in 1″ boiling salted water 20 to 45 min., until a leaf pulls away easily. Trim stem. Serve upright on individual plates as dinner appetizer or vegetable.

How to Eat Artichokes: Pull one leaf at a time from the base. Dip its tender end in melted butter and pull between your teeth to scoop out soft pulp. Discard fibrous portion of leaf. Repeat until you have eaten all the leaves. Scoop out the choke or core with a spoon and discard. Below choke is the heart or bottom; cut up heart with knife and fork, dip in butter and eat.

Celery root, also called knob celery or celeriac, has a delicate, individual flavor. It is equally delicious as a salad or vegetable.

SAUTEED CELERY ROOTS

Peel 2 large celery roots; cut into ¼″ slices (about 4 cups, cut). Add juice of 2 lemons; cover with cold water, soak 10 min. Drain and pat dry. Sauté in 3 tbsp. butter until soft and golden. Add salt and pepper to taste and 3 tbsp. chopped parsley. *6 servings.*

CELERY ROOT AND ORANGE SALAD

2 large celery roots
juice of 2 lemons
2 tbsp. salt
1 can (11 oz.) mandarin oranges
½ cup broken walnuts
⅓ cup sweet French dressing
  (add 1 tsp. poppy seeds to dressing)

Peel roots; cut in match-like strips (about 4 cups, cut). Cover with cold water, set aside. In large saucepan, bring 1 qt. water to boil. Add juice, salt, and drained celery root. Bring to boil; cook 2 to 3 min., until just tender. Drain, cool. Add oranges, nuts, and dressing; toss. Chill ½ to 1 hr. *4 servings.*

15

"In March, July, October, May—the Ides are on the fifteenth day."

16

The French serve cooked leeks with French dressing as an hors d'oeuvre.

17

The "Top o' the Morning!" to all wearers of the green.

18

"People who are not up to a thing are usually down on it."— Hubbard

19

"A parrot is for prating priz'd, but prattling women are despised."—Franklin

20

For a spring touch, sprinkle chopped chives in scrambled eggs.

21

"The woods are alive with the murmur and sound of spring."—Wilde

BUTTERMILK BREAD

Easy-to-shape loaves that are wonderful when warm.

1 cup buttermilk
3 tbsp. sugar
2½ tsp. salt
⅓ cup shortening
1 pkg. active dry yeast
1 cup warm water (not hot—
   110 to 115°)
5½ to 5¾ cups unsifted Gold
   Medal Flour
¼ tsp. soda

Scald buttermilk. Stir in sugar, salt, and shortening. Cool to lukewarm. Sprinkle yeast over warm water in mixing bowl; stir to dissolve. Add milk mixture. Add 3 cups flour, soda. Beat until smooth. Add enough remaining flour to handle easily. Turn onto lightly floured board and knead until smooth and elastic, about 10 min. Place in greased bowl, greased-side-up. Cover with cloth and let rise in warm place (85°) until double in bulk, about 1 hr., or until impression remains when touched gently with finger. (If kitchen is cool, place dough on a rack over a bowl of hot water and cover completely with a towel.)

Punch down dough, round up and let rest 15 min. on lightly floured cloth-covered board. Cut in half. Flatten each piece into an oblong, 9 x 7 x 1". Fold wide sides to center, overlapping slightly; press each end down firmly. Pinch center and ends of loaf well. Place sealed-side-down in two greased loaf pans, 8½ x 4½ x 2¾". Cover. Let rise in warm place (85°) until center is slightly higher than pan, about 1 hr.

Heat oven to 400° (mod. hot). Bake 35 to 45 min., or until well browned and sounds hollow when tapped. *Makes 2 loaves.*

22

1841—Cornstarch was patented by O. Jones.

●●

23

"All sorrows are less with bread."—Cervantes

●●

24

"It is better to wear out than to rust out."—Bishop R. Cumberland

●●

25

"All would live long, but none would be old."—Benjamin Franklin

●●

26

1953—Dr. Jonas E. Salk announced the first successful anti-polio vaccine.

●●

27

1513—Ponce de León discovered Florida in quest of the Fountain of Youth.

●●

28

1797—A washing machine was patented by Nathaniel Briggs.

The word "Lent" is an abbreviated version of the Saxon name "Lengthentide" — the time when the days lengthen.

This Lenten season discover how nutritious and good dishes featuring eggs, cheese, and sea food can be, whether you are fasting or simply seeking mealtime variety.

CREAMED CURRIED EGGS

An economical way to use hard-cooked Easter eggs.

1 can (4 oz.) sliced musrooms *or* ½ lb. fresh mushrooms, sliced
2 tbsp. butter
1 can (10½ oz.) cream of celery soup, undiluted
½ cup milk
½ to 1 tsp. curry powder
4 hard-cooked eggs, sliced
4 English muffins, cut in half, buttered and toasted

Sauté mushrooms in butter using an 8 or 9″ skillet. Mix soup, milk, and curry powder; add to mushrooms. Gently stir in eggs. Heat and serve over English muffin halves. Garnish with chopped parsley. *4 servings.*

SALMON SALAD, ISLAND-STYLE

1 can (1 lb.) salmon
1 can (13 oz.) pineapple chunks, well drained, *or* 1½ cups sweet green grapes
½ cup diced celery
2 tbsp. sweet pickle relish
½ tsp. salt
1 tbsp. prepared mustard
1 tbsp. mayonnaise
1 tbsp. French dressing
1 to 2 ripe bananas

Drain salmon; remove skin and round bones; break into chunks. Add pineapple, celery, pickle relish, and salt. Blend mustard, mayonnaise, and French dressing; mix in lightly. Slice bananas about ¼″ thick; fold in. Serve on crisp greens. *6 servings.*

Note: Tuna, cooked chicken, or veal may be used in place of salmon.

Soup and Salad Luncheon

Creamy Tomato Soup
*Salmon Salad, Island-Style
Hard Rolls, Butter
Mint-frosted Brownies

29

Grated lemon rind in French dressing adds a tangy touch.

●●●

30

1867—Bargain day! The U.S. purchased Alaska for less than 2¢ an acre.

●●●

31

"Never yet was a springtime when the buds forgot to blow."—M. E. Sangster

●●●

LOBSTER-POTATO SALAD IN THE SHELLS

Pretty enough for any party occasion. See picture on p. 72.

4 frozen lobster tails
1½ tbsp. salt
1 tbsp. sea food seasoning
4 cups cubed cold boiled potatoes
1 tbsp. finely chopped onion
½ tsp. salt
1¼ cups salad dressing
2 hard-cooked eggs, chopped
1 cup chopped unpeeled
  cucumber
2 tbsp. chopped chives

Fill large saucepan with enough water to cover lobster tails; add salt and sea food seasoning. Bring to boil. Add frozen lobster tails.

Bring to boil again and cook 15 min. Remove from water; when cool enough to handle, cut through tails lengthwise with kitchen shears. Remove membrane. Carefully remove lobster meat from shells; coarsely dice it.

Mix potatoes, onions, salt, dressing, eggs, cucumber, chives, and diced lobster meat; mix lightly. Spoon into lobster shells. Chill until serving time. Serve with wedges of lime. *4 servings.*

Use extra salad for refills.

How many million Aprils came
Before I ever knew
How white a cherry bough could be
A bed of squills, how blue!
—SARA TEASDALE

Flower: Sweet Pea or Daisy　　　　　　　**Gem:** Diamond

April's name is derived from the Latin *aperire,* meaning to open. And, in truth, April is a month of opening. It's a gardener's month, for the trees bud overhead and the bulbs at our feet open. It's a month for entertaining, and once again we open our homes to company following the austerities of Lent. April opens the fashion world, too. On Easter Sunday church steps all over the country become flower gardens of silk and satin posies bobbing atop incredible bonnets. To make your "old favorite" look like new again, try this simple perk-up operation on the veil: spread the limp veil between two pieces of

waxed paper and press gently with a warm iron. That's all there
is to it!

April foolery, which starts off the month, separates the early
birds from the sleepyheads. Jokers usually get their victims
most readily before the first cup of coffee has cleared away
morning melancholia. Just how the custom started is obscure,
but we do know that it goes back to the Romans' *Festum Fatu-
orum,* or Fools' Holiday. It may be comforting, then, for those
of us who have fallen for such trickery to know that thousands
have worn that same foolish grin long before us.

Above all, April is a month of religious significance for both
Christians and Jews; both Easter and Passover come most
often in April during this last half of the twentieth century.
Passover, or *Passach,* is the seven-day festival that recalls the
Exodus, the deliverance of the Jews from Egyptian bondage.
Easter, the Christian day of joy, commemorates the resurrec-
tion of Jesus Christ. Thus, we think of Easter as a time of
rebirth, the beginning of new life on earth.

With the earthy fragrance of newly spaded gardens, the first
concert of song sparrows returning to nest in the tulip tree, and
the matted winter lawn now turning green after a night's steady
rain, April brings to all a sharpened awareness of the natural
world around us.

A PLANT-TIMER

*Sow peason and beans, in the Wane of the Moon
Who soweth them sooner, he soweth too soon,
That they with the planet may rest and rise,
And flourish, with bearing most plentifulwise.*
—THOMAS TUSSER (1515-1580)

APRIL RED-LETTER FOODS:
CARROTS AND PINEAPPLES

TIPS ON BUYING CARROTS
1 lb. serves 4.

Fresh, bright orange, smooth, firm, clean, crisp, straight. Long, tender roots are best. Avoid green at top or soft, flabby, cracked carrots.

TIPS ON BUYING PINEAPPLES
1 medium pineapple yields 3 cups cut-up fruit.

Pineapple is ripe if top center leaves pull out easily, distinct crevices surround each section, and fruit is pliable to touch. Quality fruit is heavy for size.

Plentiful Vegetables

Asparagus
Cabbage
Carrots
Celery
Greens
Onions (Green and Dry)
Peas
Potatoes (New and Mature)
Winter Squashes

Other Available Vegetables

Artichokes
Beets (Late)
Broccoli
Cauliflower
Eggplant
Mushrooms
Parsnips
Peppers
Rutabagas
Sweet Potatoes and Yams
Turnips

Plentiful Fruits

Avocados
Cantaloupe
Grapefruit
Lemons
Oranges
Pineapples
Rhubarb
Strawberries

1

" Marked by Custom's rules, a day of being and of making Fools."

2

"He that steals an egg will steal an ox."—George Herbert

3

1860—First Pony Express started from St. Joseph, Mo., for Sacramento.

4

1802—Dorothea Dix, pioneer in mental health care, born in Hampden, Me.

5

1614—Pocahontas married John Rolfe in Jamestown, Va.

6

"Over me bright April shakes out her rain-drenched hair."—Teasdale

✿✿✿✿✿✿✿✿✿✿✿✿✿✿✿

Porch Party

*Calico Meat Loaves

Poppy Seed Noodles

Lettuce Wedges

Corn Meal Muffins

*Island Delight

✿✿✿✿✿✿✿✿✿✿✿✿✿✿✿

ISLAND DELIGHT

A refreshing fruit dessert.

10 coconut macaroons
2 cups commercial sour cream
2 tbsp. brown sugar
2 cups cubed sweetened fresh
　or canned pineapple (about
　1 medium pineapple)
1 cup sliced, drained, sweetened
　strawberries

Finely crumble macaroons into bowl; blend in sour cream and sugar. Cover and chill 2 to 3 hr. To serve: layer chilled fruits and sour cream mixture in parfait glasses or dessert dishes; serve immediately. *6 to 8 servings.*

CALICO MEAT LOAVES

1½ lb. ground beef or veal
½ lb. ground pork
3 medium slices soft bread, torn
　in pieces and ¾ cup milk *or*
　1 cup dry bread crumbs and
　1 cup milk
2 cups grated carrots (3 large)
1 egg, slightly beaten
¼ cup minced onion
1¼ tsp. salt
¼ tsp. *each* pepper, dry
　mustard, celery salt, and
　garlic salt
1 tbsp. Worcestershire sauce

Heat oven to 350° (mod.). Combine ingredients and shape mixture into 2 meat loaves. Place in large baking pan. Pour 1¼ cups Spicy Tomato Sauce (below) over loaves. Bake 1½ hr., basting occasionally with sauce. *8 servings.* Any remaining meat loaf will be delicious the second day reheated or sliced cold.

SPICY TOMATO SAUCE

1 can (6 oz.) tomato paste
3 cans water
¼ cup onion, finely chopped
1 clove garlic, minced
1 tsp. salt
⅛ tsp. pepper
¼ tsp. ground oregano
¼ tsp. basil

Combine ingredients and simmer 10 min. *Makes 2½ cups.* Refrigerate remaining sauce for use on hamburgers, franks, etc.

7

Fresh mint and pineapple are perfect mates.

▲▲▲

8

1873—Oleomargarine patented by A. Paraf of New York.

▲▲▲

9

1865—General Robert E. Lee surrendered at Appomattox, Va.

▲▲▲

10

To glaze cooked carrots, simmer in butter, sugar, and mint jelly.

▲▲▲

11

"The stomach supports the heart, and not the heart the stomach."—Proverb

▲▲▲

12

1912—Clara Barton, first president of the American Red Cross, died.

▲▲▲

13

1743—Thomas Jefferson born in Shadwell, Va.

✧⟩✧⟩✧⟩✧⟩✧⟩✧⟩✧⟩✧⟩✧⟩✧⟩✧⟩

Dinner for Honored Guests

Broiled Sirloin Steaks

Sautéed Mushrooms

Hash Brown Potatoes

Broccoli   Hot Rolls

*Crunchy Carrot-Pineapple Mold

Lemon Meringue Pie

✧⟩✧⟩✧⟩✧⟩✧⟩✧⟩✧⟩✧⟩✧⟩✧⟩✧⟩

CRUNCHY CARROT-PINEAPPLE MOLD

1 can (1 lb. 12 oz.) crushed
   pineapple (3½ cups)
1 cup water
1 pkg. (3 oz.) lemon-flavored
   gelatin
1 pkg. (3 oz.) orange-flavored
   gelatin
1 cup finely diced celery
1 cup grated carrots
¾ cup chopped nuts
2 cups (1 lb.) fine curd cottage
   cheese
1 cup whipping cream, whipped
½ cup mayonnaise

Heat pineapple and water to boiling. Add gelatin and stir until dissolved. Chill until partially thickened. Fold in remaining ingredients; turn into 16 individual molds or two 1-qt. molds. Chill until firm. *16 servings.*

CREAMY VEGETABLE-BEEF CASSEROLE

A festive version of beef stew.

1½ lb. stewing beef, cubed
½ cup seasoned Bisquick
½ cup cooked tomatoes
2 small onions, chopped
3 large carrots, sliced
1 small clove garlic, cut up
⅔ cup commercial sour cream
¼ tsp. Worcestershire sauce
Chive Biscuits (below)

Roll beef in Bisquick seasoned with salt, pepper, and paprika. Brown meat thoroughly on all sides in hot fat. Add vegetables and garlic; sauté until onions are transparent. Add enough water to cover meat and vegetables. Cover tightly and cook over low heat until meat is tender, 1½ to 2 hr. Add more water during cooking, if necessary. Stir in sour cream, Worcestershire sauce, salt, and pepper to taste.

Heat oven to 425° (hot). Pour stew into 2-qt. baking dish and cover hot mixture with Chive Biscuits. Bake 15 to 20 min. *4 to 6 servings.*

Chive Biscuits: Add ⅔ cup commercial sour cream, ⅓ cup water, and 1 tbsp. chopped chives all at once to 2 cups Bisquick. Beat hard 20 strokes; knead 8 to 10 times. Cut about 12 biscuits.

14

1828—Webster's "Dictionary of the English Language" published.

15

1865—Abraham Lincoln assassinated.

16

For variety, cut carrots in circles, sticks, chunks, or diagonally.

17

1790—Benjamin Franklin died in Philadelphia at the age of 84.

18

1775—Paul Revere's midnight ride for liberty.

19

1892—C. E. Duryea drove the first practical automobile in Springfield, Mass.

20

Add garlic croutons to cream of tomato soup.

❀⟩❀⟩❀⟩❀⟩❀⟩❀⟩❀⟩❀⟩❀⟩❀⟩❀⟩❀⟩❀⟩

Luncheon Before Bridge

Clam Juice Cocktail
*Fonduloha
Melba Toast and Rye Rounds
Chocolate Sundae Tarts

❀⟩❀⟩❀⟩❀⟩❀⟩❀⟩❀⟩❀⟩❀⟩❀⟩❀⟩❀⟩❀⟩

FONDULOHA

Chicken salad in pineapple boats.

**2 fresh pineapples
2½ cups diced cooked chicken
or turkey
¾ cup diced celery
¾ cup sliced bananas
⅓ cup salted peanuts
¾ cup mayonnaise
2 tbsp. chutney *or* ½ tsp. salt
and ¼ tsp. pepper
½ to 1 tsp. curry powder
½ cup shredded coconut
mandarin oranges**

Cut pineapples into quarters lengthwise, leaving green tops on. Cut around edges with curved knife, remove fruit, and dice. Drain pineapples and pineapple shells very well on absorbent paper. Combine pineapple, chicken, celery, bananas, and peanuts in 3-qt. mixing bowl. In small bowl, blend mayonnaise, chutney, and curry. Lightly toss mayonnaise mixture with pineapple mixture. Fill pineapple shells. Garnish with shredded coconut and mandarin oranges. *8 servings.*

CARROTS AU GRATIN

A delicious way of serving colorful vitamin-rich carrots.

**3 cups diced carrots
6 soda crackers, crushed
(¼ cup)
1 tsp. onion salt
¼ cup chopped green pepper
dash of pepper
2 tbsp. melted butter
½ cup grated sharp cheese**

Cook carrots in ½″ boiling salted water 10 min., or until tender. Heat oven to 425° (hot). Combine cracker crumbs, onion salt, green pepper, and pepper. Alternate layers of carrots and crumb mixture in greased 1-qt. baking dish. Spoon on any remaining carrot liquid. Pour on butter and sprinkle with cheese. Bake 15 to 20 min., or until cheese melts. *6 servings.*

Cutting Fresh Pineapple

Cut off top and bottom. To remove rind, cut down length in wide strokes.

Cut V-shaped wedges full length of diagonal "eyes." Discard.

Cut across in slices or lengthwise in spears; remove core.

21

"Economy is too late at the bottom of the purse."—Seneca

22

Colorful salad: fresh pineapple chunks with cubes of jellied cranberry.

23

Cooked carrots are delicious dusted with nutmeg or cinnamon.

24

1833—Soda fountain patented by Jacob Elbert of Cadiz, Ohio.

25

1901—First automobile license plates issued, in New York State.

26

"There is no love sincerer than the love of food."—George Bernard Shaw

27

"Forty is the age of youth; fifty is the youth of age."—French Proverb

EASTER HAM

Ham is as much a part of Easter for grown-ups as is the Easter bunny for small fry. And after starring at the Easter dinner table, ham lends itself to a myriad of delicious dishes, such as the Ham-Onion-Broccoli Casserole on p. 10.

Heat oven to 325° (slow mod.). Place meat fat-side-up on rack in pan. Insert meat thermometer into center of thickest muscle. Do not cover. Do not add water.

	Weight	Time
Ham	4 lb.	2½ hr.
	6 lb.	3¼ hr.
	8 lb.	3½ hr.
	10 lb.	3¾ hr.
	12 lb.	4 hr.
	14 lb.	4¼ hr.
Picnic	6 lb.	3 hr.
	8 lb.	4 hr.
Shoulder butt	2 lb.	2 hr.
	4 lb.	4 hr.

Roast ham to an internal temperature of 160°, picnic and shoulder butt to 170°.

Half an hour before ham is done, take from oven and remove rind. Score by cutting fat into diamond shapes. Insert whole cloves. Cover with a sweet glaze (right). Return to 400° (mod. hot) oven for browning. Let ham rest 15 to 20 min. before carving.

◊﹥◊﹥◊﹥◊﹥◊﹥◊﹥◊﹥◊﹥◊﹥◊﹥◊﹥

Family Easter Dinner

*Fruit-glazed Easter Ham
Baked Sweet Potatoes
Broccoli with Hollandaise Sauce
Iced Relishes   Cloverleaf Rolls
Orange-Pineapple Angel Food Cake

◊﹥◊﹥◊﹥◊﹥◊﹥◊﹥◊﹥◊﹥◊﹥◊﹥◊﹥

Apricot Glaze: Mix 1 cup apricot jam and ⅓ cup honey. Spread over ham after scoring.

Cranberry Glaze: Combine 1 cup brown sugar (packed) and 1 tbsp. dry mustard. Add ½ cup bottled cranberry cocktail. Spoon over ham after scoring.

Pineapple Glaze: Combine 1 cup pineapple juice, 1 cup brown sugar (packed), 4 tsp. prepared mustard, and 2 to 3 tbsp. lemon juice. Glaze ham after scoring.

28

Color note for cole slaw: chopped carrots or sliced green olives.

▲▲

29

Soften brown sugar by storing in tight container with apple slices.

▲▲

30

1789—George Washington inaugurated as first president of the U. S.

▲▲

Nature Outdoes Us

While we may dye eggs a myriad of colors, nature tops us by varying their shapes and sizes as well as their colors. Eggs are white, beige, green, blue, pink, spotted, and mottled. They are pear-shaped, like the plover's eggs; cylindrical, like the sand grouse's; and round, like the owl's. Sizes vary from the hummingbird's eggs, no larger than the tip of your little finger, to the extinct Aepyornis' eggs, with a volume of more than 2 gallons.

Hail, beauteous May, that doth inspire
Mirth, and youth, and warm desire;
Woods and groves are of thy dressing,
Hill and dale doth boast thy blessing.
—JOHN MILTON

Flower: Hawthorn or Lily of the Valley   **Gem:** Emerald

The month of May took its name from Maia, the Roman goddess of growth—and a most appropriate derivation! Here, on all sides, are the flowers that the April rains promised: dogwood, hawthorn, and silver bells; the flaming azaleas and rhododendron; flowering quince and borders iridescent with early perennials and late bulbs.

But don't leave all your May flowers outside. It's fun to have bowls of bloom about the house, even in the bathroom. Use a prized cup that has lost its saucer, a seldom-used teapot, or perhaps a squatty little antique sugar bowl. Floating blossoms are pretty, too, especially in unusual containers—perhaps a bon-bon dish or a fancy ash tray. For conventional arrangements, however, you'll want cut flowers. If you cut them on a slant with a sharp knife at a cool time of day, and then put them into tepid water (100°) for an hour before arranging them in a vase of cold water, you'll find that they'll keep much longer.

In sixteenth-century England, the young at heart would rise before dawn on the first day of May and flock to the woods to gather blossoms. At sunrise, they would return to the village to decorate doors and windows and the Maypole which was set up in the square. The choicest blooms were fashioned into a crown for the local beauty who was proclaimed Queen of the May. Both of these traditions still survive in some form in contemporary American life. While the younger girls make flower baskets to leave at friends' doors, their college-age sisters preserve the traditional crowning of the May Queen ceremony.

Mothers will have their day this month. Anna Jarvis of Philadelphia first conceived of the idea for a Mother's Day in 1907, and it was first celebrated on May 10 of the following year. President Woodrow Wilson issued the proclamation which fixed this day on the second Sunday of the month.

May brings Memorial Day, too. This is most welcome, since it is the first of the warm-weather holidays. Originated in 1868 lest the "ravages of time testify to coming generations that we have forgotten as a people the cost of a free and undivided government," Memorial Day now honors the dead of all wars.

A 1609 FRECKLE REMEDY

Wash your face in the wane of the moone with a spunge, morninge and euening, with a water distilled in Maie of Elder Leaues, letting the same drie into the skinne.

MAY RED-LETTER FOODS:
ASPARAGUS AND RHUBARB

Plentiful Vegetables	*Other Available Vegetables*	*Plentiful Fruits*
Asparagus	Artichokes	Bananas
Cabbage	Beets (Late)	Cantaloupe and
Carrots	Corn	Casaba Melons
Celery	Peppers	Cherries
Eggplant	Sweet Potatoes	Grapefruit
Greens	and Yams	Lemons
Mushrooms	Turnips	Oranges
Onions (Green		Pineapples
and Dry)		Rhubarb
Peas		Strawberries
Potatoes (New		
and Mature)		

TIPS ON BUYING ASPARAGUS
About 20 stalks per lb.

Choose unbroken tips; fresh, green stalks that are straight and 6 to 10″ long. Brittle. No thin, wilted, old, tough, or woody stalks. To prevent drying, store in moisture-proof bag in refrigerator.

TIPS ON BUYING RHUBARB
1 lb. makes 2 cups sauce.

Firm, crisp, tender; pink or red. Thick stalks. Younger stems are tender and delicate. Leaves not edible. Store in refrigerator or cool, dry place.

1

The day to hang flowers on a loved one's door.

2

Sprinkle grated Parmesan cheese over hot buttered asparagus.

3

"Rains of love be sweeter far than all other pleasures are."—Dryden

4

Marinated artichoke hearts in a green salad are delicious.

5

"Hard is his herte that loveth naught in May."—Chaucer

6

1851—First mechanical refrigerator patented by Dr. John Gorrie.

7

"Great minds have purposes, others have wishes."—Washington Irving

◊>◊>◊>◊>◊>◊>◊>◊>◊>◊>◊>◊>◊>

Fancy Fixin's

Beef Tenderloin
with Sliced Mushrooms

Brown Rice with Almonds

*Asparagus à la Polonaise

Tossed Green Salad

Dinner Rolls

Cantaloupe

◊>◊>◊>◊>◊>◊>◊>◊>◊>◊>◊>◊>◊>

ASPARAGUS
A LA POLONAISE

2 lb. fresh asparagus
⅓ cup butter
⅓ cup soft bread cubes
2 hard-cooked eggs, finely
  chopped
1 tbsp. chopped parsley
salt and pepper to taste

Prepare asparagus by breaking off tough ends. Wash well. Tie in bunches; cook upright in narrow deep pan or coffeepot. Simmer in 1″ salted water partially covered 2 min.; then covered 8 to 15 min. until tender. Catch string with fork when lifting out. Meanwhile, melt butter until foamy. Stir in bread cubes and cook over low heat until crisp and golden brown. Remove from heat. Add rest of ingredients. Serve over cooked asparagus. *4 to 6 servings.*

CHICKEN-ASPARAGUS-CHEESE BAKE

Flavor-rich and savory. This golden "bake" needs only a salad accompaniment.

1 lb. fresh asparagus, cut up
  and cooked, *or* 1 pkg. frozen
  cut-up asparagus, cooked
2 cups sliced cooked chicken
½ tsp. *each* marjoram and sage
1 cup unsifted Gold Medal Flour
2 tsp. baking powder
1 tsp. salt
2 eggs, beaten
½ cup milk
1 cup grated Cheddar cheese
Cheese Sauce (p. 157)

Heat oven to 350° (mod.). Line 11½ x 7½ x 1½″ baking dish with layer of asparagus. Place chicken atop asparagus. Sprinkle herbs over chicken. Stir flour, baking powder, and salt together in mixing bowl. Beat eggs, milk, and cheese; add to flour mixture. Beat batter well and pour over chicken, spreading evenly. Bake 25 to 30 min. Cut into squares and serve hot with Cheese Sauce. *6 servings.*

8

Easy sundae: vanilla ice cream with pecan halves and honey.

9

"Sum up at night, what thou hast done by day."—George Herbert

10

1899—Fred Astaire, American dancer and actor, born in Omaha, Nebraska.

11

"God can't be always everywhere: and so, invented Mothers."—Edwin Arnold

12

1914—Mother's Day was first nationally observed.

13

"It's easier to be wise for others than for ourselves."—La Rochefoucauld

14

For variety, serve asparagus with grated nutmeg or prepared mustard.

✿✦✿✦✿✦✿✦✿✦✿✦✿✦✿✦✿✦✿

Woman's Club Luncheon

*Vinaigrette Vegetable Plate
Tiny Hot Cheese Biscuits
Meringues with Raspberry Sherbet

✿✦✿✦✿✦✿✦✿✦✿✦✿✦✿✦✿✦✿

VEGETABLES VINAIGRETTE

1 lb. fresh asparagus *or*
   1 lb. fresh whole green beans
1 head fresh cauliflower *or*
   1 pkg. frozen cauliflower
1 can (7 oz.) artichoke hearts
Vinaigrette Dressing (below)

Cook asparagus or beans and cauliflower. Drain artichokes. Pour ¼ cup Vinaigrette Dressing over each vegetable. Chill at least 1 hr. Arrange the three vegetables artistically on individual serving plates or on one large platter. Garnish with cherry tomatoes or parsley. *4 servings.*

Vinaigrette Dressing: Mix 1 cup oil-and-vinegar dressing, 2 tbsp. chopped parsley, ¼ cup finely chopped pickle, 2 tsp. chopped onion, and, if desired, 2 tsp. capers. *1½ cups.*

Vinaigrette Vegetable Plate: Serve Vegetables Vinaigrette with large cooked shrimp dipped in rich mayonnaise.

SHRIMP AND ASPARAGUS CASSEROLE

Colorful and rich luncheon dish. Serve with salad, rolls, and spicy fruit pie.

1 cup rice, cooked
1 lb. fresh asparagus, cut
   up and cooked, *or* 1 pkg. frozen cut-up asparagus, cooked
3 cans (4½ oz. each) shrimp
2 tbsp. butter
2 tbsp. flour
1¼ cups milk
½ lb. sharp Cheddar cheese,
   grated
salt and paprika

Heat oven to 350° (mod.). Spread rice in buttered baking dish, 11½ x 7½ x 1½". Spread asparagus over rice. Cover with shrimp. Melt butter, stir in flour; cook over low heat, stirring until mixture is smooth, bubbly. Remove from heat. Stir in milk and cheese. Bring to boil; boil 1 min., stirring constantly. Season to taste with salt and paprika. Pour sauce over shrimp in baking dish. Sprinkle with paprika. Bake 20 min. *6 to 8 servings.*

15

1940—Nylon stockings went on sale for the first time.

16

1929—First "Oscars" awarded, to Janet Gaynor and Emil Jannings.

17

"Let all thy Joys be as the month of May."—Francis Quarles

18

1860—Abraham Lincoln nominated at Republican Convention in Chicago.

19

"Tale-bearers are as bad as tale-makers."—Sheridan

20

May fruit plate idea: pitted Bing cherries filled with cream cheese.

21

1927—Charles Lindbergh completed first trans-Atlantic solo flight in Paris.

⊙⟩⊙⟩⊙⟩⊙⟩⊙⟩⊙⟩⊙⟩⊙⟩⊙⟩⊙⟩

Quick and Easy Dinner

Broiled Lamb Chops, Mint Jelly

French Fried Potatoes

Buttered Carrots

Tossed Salad

Crisp Bread Sticks

*Rhubarb Ice Cream

⊙⟩⊙⟩⊙⟩⊙⟩⊙⟩⊙⟩⊙⟩⊙⟩⊙⟩⊙⟩

RHUBARB ICE CREAM

2 cups diced pink rhubarb
1 cup water
1 cup sugar
1 tbsp. lemon juice
3 drops red food coloring
1 egg white, stiffly beaten†
1 cup whipping cream, whipped

In saucepan, combine rhubarb, water, and sugar. Boil 10 to 12 min., until sauce-like. Cool; blend in lemon juice and food coloring. Pour into refrigerator tray and freeze to a mush, 1 to 2 hr. Remove from freezer and gradually add to beaten egg white, beating on low speed on mixer until rhubarb mush and egg white are blended. Fold in whipped cream. Return to freezing trays (fills 2 trays ⅔ full). Freeze 2 hr. before serving. *12 servings.*

† *See page 172*

RHUBARB-ORANGE PIE

8″ Baked Pie Shell
¼ cup orange juice
3 cups rhubarb, cut in 1″ pieces
1½ cups granulated sugar
¼ cup cornstarch
2 egg yolks
2 tbsp. butter
1 tbsp. grated orange rind
3 to 4 drops red food coloring
½ cup whipping cream
2 tbsp. confectioners' sugar
½ tsp. vanilla

Combine orange juice and rhubarb in saucepan. Cover and cook over medium heat until mixture boils; boil 1 min. Remove from heat. Combine sugar with cornstarch; blend into rhubarb mixture. Beat egg yolks slightly; blend into mixture. Return to heat, bring to boil and boil 4 min. Remove from heat; stir in butter, orange rind, and food coloring. Cool. Pour into cooled baked pie shell. Chill until ready to serve. Whip cream until stiff. Fold in confectioners' sugar and vanilla. Spoon on pie just before serving.

22

"A swarm of bees in May is worth a load of hay."—English Proverb

23

1868—Kit Carson, scout and pioneer of the West, died in Colorado.

24

1883—"Eighth Wonder of the World," the Brooklyn Bridge, opened.

25

"Hope is a light diet, but a very stimulating one."—Balzac

26

To sliver nuts, blanch and cut with sharp knife while warm and moist.

27

1818—Amelia Bloomer, suffragette and fashion innovator, born.

28

Cherries are an attractive garnish for any fruit salad or dessert.

ROAST LAMB

French leg of lamb, glazed with currant jelly, is pictured on pp. 70-71.

Heat oven to 325° (slow mod.). Season meat with salt and pepper. For special flavor, cut slits in roast with tip of knife and insert sliver of garlic or rub marjoram, thyme, or rosemary into surface of roast. Place fat-side-up on rack in open pan. Insert meat thermometer into thickest part of meat.

Roast meat. Do not baste, do not cover, do not add water. If desired, glaze with currant jelly.

	Min. per lb.	Meat temp.
Leg**	30-35	175-180°
Shoulder		
Square cut	30-35	175-180°
Rolled	40-45	175-180°
Cushion	30-35	175-180°

After roasting, let meat rest in warm place 15 to 20 min. for easiest carving.

**The French prefer their lamb a delicate pink. If you'd like to try it, roast leg of lamb 25 min. per lb., 170° meat temperature.

◑➤◐➤◑➤◐➤◑➤◐➤◑➤◐➤◑➤◐➤◑➤◐➤◑

Saturday Night Dinner Party

Fresh Fruit Cup

*Roast Lamb

New Potatoes in the Jackets

Fresh Asparagus Almondine

Tomato Aspic Ring with Water Cress

Herb Biscuits

Rhubarb-Orange Pie (p. 64)

◑➤◐➤◑➤◐➤◑➤◐➤◑➤◐➤◑➤◐➤◑➤◐➤◑

ROAST LAMB

Hot on Sunday
Cold on Monday
Hashed on Tuesday
Minced on Wednesday
Curry Thursday
Broth on Friday
Pie on Saturday

29

1953—Highest point on earth, Mount Everest, conquered by man.

•–•

30

Memorial Day, a holiday in most states.

•–•

31

1889—2,000 lives lost in the Great Johnstown (Pa.) Flood.

•–•

SPRING CHIVE SAUCE

Should there be some lamb left over, serve it cold, in the Old English tradition, with this sauce.

2 hard-cooked eggs, very finely chopped
3 tbsp. vegetable oil
3 tbsp. finely chopped chives
1 tbsp. sugar
1½ tsp. salt
¼ to ½ tsp. black pepper
¼ cup vinegar
3 tbsp. water

Combine chopped eggs and oil. Add remaining ingredients and stir well. Chill. Also delicious as a dressing for a salad of tossed vegetables or greens.

THURSDAY LAMB CURRY

3 large apples, pared, cored, and sliced
1 onion, sliced
1 clove garlic
2 to 3 tbsp. flour
1 tbsp. curry powder
1 tbsp. lemon juice
2 cups meat stock or bouillon
1 tsp. gravy flavoring
grated rind of ½ lemon
½ cup raisins
3 whole cloves
2 cups cubed leftover cooked lamb

Sauté apples, onion, and garlic in butter until golden brown. Remove garlic. Blend in flour and curry powder. Combine lemon juice, stock, and gravy flavoring; stir in gradually. Stir in lemon rind, raisins, and cloves. Cover, simmer 30 min. Add lamb. Heat. Serve with rice and chutney. *6 servings.*

WEDDING ANNIVERSARY GIFT CHART

Whether it is the first or the fiftieth, a wedding anniversary calls for a celebration. Remembering their marriage dates, and signifying the exact number of years with an appropriate gift, will help to show your affection for close friends and relatives.

> *Marriage resembles a pair of shears, so joined that they can not be separated; often moving in opposite directions, yet always punishing anyone who comes between them.*
>
> —SIDNEY SMITH

1st	paper	13th	lace
2nd	cotton	14th	ivory
3rd	leather	15th	crystal
4th	silk, fruit, flowers	20th	china
5th	wood	25th	silver
6th	iron	30th	pearl
7th	copper, bronze, brass	35th	coral
8th	electrical appliances	40th	ruby
9th	pottery	50th	gold
10th	tin, aluminum	55th	emerald
11th	steel	60th } 75th }	diamond
12th	linen		

> *Some pray to marry the man they love,*
> *My prayer will somewhat vary:*
> *I humbly pray to Heaven above*
> *That I love the man I marry.*
>
> —ROSE PASTOR STOKES

See page 80 →

Spring

See page 66

Some Uses for Herbs

HERB	SOUP	FISH	MEAT, EGGS	VEGETABLES
Basil	Pea, Fish Tomato Vegetable	All Baked and Broiled Fish Shrimp	Beef, Pork Sausage Omelets	Tomato Peas Eggplant
Dill	Creamed Fish Soup Vegetable	All Broiled Fish Shrimp Fish Sauces	Lamb Chops Roasts, Steaks Corned Beef	Green Beans Cabbage Cauliflower
Marjoram	Potato Vegetable Chowder	All Baked Fish Creamed Fish Sauces	Hash Stuffing Lamb, Beef	Carrots Salads Spinach
Oregano	Bean Lentil Chowder	All Baked Fish Shrimp Lobster	Meat Pies Veal, Pork Baked Eggs	Tomato Green Beans Onions
Rosemary	Minestrone Chicken Pea	All Strong- flavored Fish Salmon	Veal, Pork Lamb, Beef Deviled Eggs	Cauliflower Mushrooms Peas
Sage		Stuffing	Pork, Lamb Sausages Veal	Tomato Beans Onions
Savory	Vegetable Chowder Bean, Pea	All Shellfish and Fish Stuffing	All Meats All Egg Dishes Poultry	Cabbage Peas Beans
Tarragon	Chicken Fish Mushroom	All Shellfish All Barbecued Fish Marinades	Scrambled Eggs Chicken Rabbit, Veal	Mushrooms Salads Marinades
Thyme	Chicken Chowder Stews	All Shellfish and Fish Fish Sauces	Beef, Lamb Pork, Veal Game, Eggs	Beets Onions Beans

← *See page 43*

*My luve is like a red, red rose
That's newly sprung in June.*
—ROBERT BURNS

Flower: Rose   **Gem:** Pearl or Moonstone

June is rose month, the flower's shining hour. Cabbage, moss, yellowbrier, damask, rambler, and everblooming—all these varieties do their fragrant best to let your June yard live up to the lyric "bustin' out all over." The early Romans were known to be particular rose lovers. Their banquet couches were strewn with the delicate petals—hence the expression, "bed of roses"; the Roman Code of Law prohibited anything said under a garland of roses at a dinner or meeting from being repeated in court —thus, "sub rosa."

You may want to keep a fragrant year-round reminder of this gentle month by making this old-fashioned rose petal potpourri:

> Gather fragrant rose petals in the early morning, spread on paper and dry in a dark, cool place for a week. To each 4 cups of dried petals, add 1 tsp. each of powdered orris root, ground cinnamon, nutmeg, cloves, and the rinds of one lemon and orange, dried and crushed. Mix thoroughly. Store in a pretty jar, sprinkling coarse salt on each layer of spiced petals. Close tightly for 6 weeks. To release fragrance, open jar and stir.

The month takes its name from the Roman goddess Juno, patroness of marriage and the special guardian of women and childbirth. It does seem fitting, then, that we should give a nod to our husbands and fathers on the second Sunday of the month, Father's Day. It was celebrated for the first time on June 19, 1910, in Spokane, Washington, under the sponsorship of the local YMCA and Ministerial Association. But the idea for such a special day was sparked by a local woman, a loving wife, Mrs. John Bruce Dodd.

June is the month of long twilights. By the 21st, the first day of summer, when the sun has moved as far north of the equator as possible, the balmy evenings are a delightful invitation to dine out of doors. Too many of us overlook the potentialities of our yards and gardens, letting them serve only as settings for our homes instead of making them into backgrounds for living. A simple portable grill on the patio is all the foundation you need for cooking and entertaining in your own backyard, and it will give you an extra dimension in gracious living.

A Flag for Flag Day

If you do not have a flag already, get one and fly it on occasions other than Flag Day, June 14: Independence Day, Labor Day, Constitution Day (Sept. 17), Columbus Day (Oct. 12), Veterans' Day (Nov. 11), Thanksgiving, Inauguration Day, Lincoln's and Washington's Birthdays, Memorial Day, and state holidays.

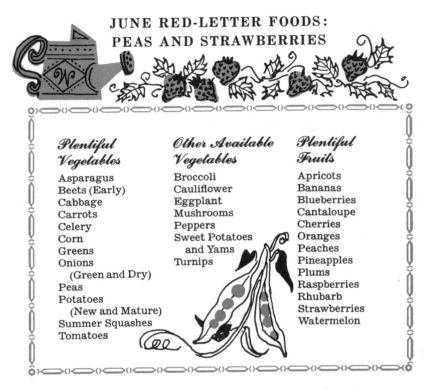

JUNE RED-LETTER FOODS:
PEAS AND STRAWBERRIES

Plentiful Vegetables	*Other Available Vegetables*	*Plentiful Fruits*
Asparagus	Broccoli	Apricots
Beets (Early)	Cauliflower	Bananas
Cabbage	Eggplant	Blueberries
Carrots	Mushrooms	Cantaloupe
Celery	Peppers	Cherries
Corn	Sweet Potatoes	Oranges
Greens	and Yams	Peaches
Onions	Turnips	Pineapples
(Green and Dry)		Plums
Peas		Raspberries
Potatoes		Rhubarb
(New and Mature)		Strawberries
Summer Squashes		Watermelon
Tomatoes		

TIPS ON BUYING PEAS
1 to 1½ lb. serves 2.

Select young peas in crisp, green, well-filled pods; no swollen pods or poor color. A fresh pea crushes easily between the fingers. Store in hydrator or plastic bag in refrigerator.

TIPS ON BUYING STRAWBERRIES
1 qt. yields 3 cups or 5 to 6 servings.

Select bright, clean, fresh, fragrant, medium-sized, tart, well-shaped strawberries with green caps. They are highly perishable. Pick over carefully, spread on tray, refrigerate a short time. For best flavor and texture, do not wash until just before using.

1

Freeze whole strawberries in ice cubes; serve in fruit drinks.

2

1953—Elizabeth II crowned at Westminster Abbey.

3

1851—New York Knickerbockers wore the first baseball uniforms.

4

"The Rose is fairest when 'tis budding new."—Sir Walter Scott

5

1752—Genesis of the lightning rod: Franklin launched his kite.

6

1882—Electric flatiron patented by Henry W. Sealey of New York.

7

Try garlic salt on hot, buttered fresh green peas.

‑O﹜O﹜O﹜O﹜O﹜O﹜O﹜O﹜O﹜O﹜O﹜O﹜

Meeting of the Gourmet Club

Jellied Madrilene

*Veal Smitane

*Peas, French-Style

Braised Celery

Popovers

Sliced Sweetened Strawberries

with Sour Cream

Demitasse

‑O﹜O﹜O﹜O﹜O﹜O﹜O﹜O﹜O﹜O﹜O﹜O﹜

PEAS, FRENCH-STYLE

Shell 3 lb. fresh peas (yields about 3 cups). Line bottom and sides of heavy saucepan with washed lettuce leaves. Add peas. Sprinkle with ½ tsp. salt, a dash each of pepper, nutmeg, and sugar; add ¼ cup butter. Cover with lettuce leaves. Cook covered over low heat about 25 min., or until tender. Discard leaves. *6 servings.*

NEW PEAS IN CREAM

Another wonderful way of serving garden-fresh peas.

Cook 2 cups fresh peas (2 lb. unshelled). Drain. Add 1 tsp. sugar, ½ tsp. salt, 2 tbsp. butter, ⅛ tsp. pepper, and ½ cup cream (20% butterfat). Heat. *4 servings.*

VEAL SMITANE

1 chicken bouillon cube
⅔ cup boiling water
1 medium onion, minced
2 tbsp. butter
1 tbsp. shortening
4 thinly sliced veal shoulder
  chops *or* 6 veal cutlets *or* 1½
  lb. veal round
¾ cup commercial sour cream
1 can (7 oz.) mushrooms,
  drained
1½ tsp. salt
¼ tsp. white pepper
1 tsp. paprika
1 tsp. dried dill leaves
two 1" strips lemon peel

Dissolve chicken bouillon cube in boiling water; set aside. Using 12" skillet, saute onion in butter until transparent; remove from skillet. Add shortening to skillet and slowly brown veal over low heat, until deeply browned. Slowly blend bouillon into sour cream. Combine with onions, mushrooms, and seasonings; pour over meat. Cover and simmer 30 min., or until meat is tender. Remove cover and simmer until gravy is desired consistency. *4 to 6 servings.*

Pork Smitane: Use 4 pork shoulder or loin chops in place of veal.

8

1869—First vacuum cleaner, a "sweeping machine," patented.

9

1791—"Home Sweet Home" author, John Howard Payne, born in New York.

10

"Seek roses in December, ice in June."—Lord Byron

11

Kamehameha Day, our 50th State honors its great 19th-century king.

12

Sautéed mushrooms or tiny green onions are good mixed with peas.

13

"Hail the bridegroom, hail the bride, when the nuptial knot is tied."—Gilbert

14

Flag Day. In 1777, the Continental Congress adopted the Stars and Stripes.

Graduation Dinner

Roast Turkey (p. 172)

Dressing   Turkey Gravy

Mashed Potatoes

Jellied Cranberries

*Pickled Beets   Stuffed Celery

Corn Sticks

*Fruit Platter Pie

PICKLED BEETS

Cook 1 lb. fresh beets in 1" boiling salted water 30 to 45 min. Drain, cool, peel, and cut up. Combine 1 cup water, ½ cup vinegar, 1 cup sugar, and 1 stick cinnamon in saucepan; bring to boil. Pour over beets. Marinate several hours or overnight in refrigerator. Pour off part of liquid when served. *Makes about 2 cups.*

FRUIT PLATTER PIE

See picture on p. 69.

1 cup unsifted Gold Medal Flour
½ tsp. salt
⅓ cup lard *or* ⅓ cup plus 1 tbsp. hydrogenated shortening
⅓ to ½ cup grated sharp Cheddar cheese
2 tbsp. water
2 to 3 cups fresh or drained canned fruit (such as sliced strawberries, pineapple chunks, mandarin oranges, banana, peach, or apple slices)
1 to 2 tbsp. sugar
Orange Sauce (below)

Heat oven to 475° (very hot). Mix flour and salt. Cut in shortening and cheese. Sprinkle with water; mix with fork. Round into ball. Roll into 13 to 14" circle on lightly floured cloth-covered board. Transfer to baking sheet, turn up edge 1" and flute. Prick. Bake 8 to 10 min. Cool.

Arrange fruit on pastry. Sprinkle with sugar. Spoon ½ cup Orange Sauce over fruit. Serve in wedges with whipped cream and additional sauce. *12 to 14 servings.*

Orange Sauce: Mix ½ cup sugar, ⅛ tsp. salt, and 1 tbsp. cornstarch in saucepan. Stir in ½ cup orange juice, 2 tbsp. lemon juice, and ¼ cup plus 2 tbsp. boiling water. Bring to boil and boil 1 min.; stir constantly. Cool.

15

Mound cantaloupe halves with blueberries for a festive breakfast fruit.

16

Rhubarb, botanically a vegetable, is cooked and served as a fruit.

17

Now is the time to put up strawberry jam for next winter's enjoyment.

18

1873—Susan B. Anthony fined $100 for trying to vote in Rochester, N. Y.

19

1885—"Lady Liberty" arrived from France to light our way.

20

1819—The steamship "Savannah" crossed the Atlantic in 26 days.

21

Summer begins: "Summer redundant, blueness abundant."—Browning

ↂↂↂↂↂↂↂↂↂↂↂ

Supper Under a Shade Tree

Cold Sliced Ham

*Summer Macaroni Salad

Toasted English Muffins

Praline Strawberry Shortcake (p. 84)

ↂↂↂↂↂↂↂↂↂↂↂ

SUMMER MACARONI SALAD

7 or 8 oz. elbow, shell, or ring
   macaroni
2 cups fresh peas
1 cup cubed Cheddar cheese
1 cup sliced gherkins
½ cup minced onion
½ cup mayonnaise

Cook, drain, and cool macaroni and peas. Add cheese, gherkins, onion, and mayonnaise. Season with salt and pepper to taste. Chill. Serve on crisp greens. *6 to 8 servings.*

ICE CREAM WITH CHERRY KABOBS

Scoop peppermint ice cream into sherbet glasses and freeze until very hard. Make kabobs by putting 2 or 3 dark sweet fresh cherries on wooden skewers. To serve: stick 1 or 2 kabobs into ice cream so kabob stands up at an angle. To eat: slip cherries off skewer onto ice cream.

Pineapple Kabobs: Use chunks of fresh or canned pineapple in place of cherries.

BING CHERRY SAUCE

A delightful ice cream topping.

2 unpeeled medium oranges,
   thinly sliced
2 cups water
4 cups fresh Bing cherries,
   pitted
3 cups sugar
¼ cup lemon juice
slivered almonds

Quarter orange slices. Combine with water in 2½-qt. pan; bring to boil. Simmer uncovered 10 min., until rind is tender. Add cherries, sugar, and lemon juice; gently simmer uncovered and stir occasionally, until syrupy, 1½ to 2 hr. Chill thoroughly. Serve over ice cream; sprinkle with slivered almonds. *Makes 2 pints.* Will keep in covered jar in refrigerator 3 to 4 weeks.

22

Children love green peas served in nests of hot shredded carrots.

~~~~~~

23

A summer sky of dazzling blue will follow morning's heavy dew.

~~~~~~

24

"Light supper maketh long life."—English Proverb

~~~~~~

25

1876—Custer's Last Stand: "Comanche," a horse, was the only survivor.

~~~~~~

26

1870—Atlantic City opened its famous boardwalk, first in the world.

~~~~~~

27

1880—Helen Keller born in Tuscumbia, Alabama.

~~~~~~

28

1778—"Molly Pitcher" hailed as heroine of the battle of Monmouth.

June brings strawberries, those heart-shaped bites of sweetness. You'll probably want to try them in new recipes like these.

OLD-FASHIONED STRAWBERRY SAUCE

Wash, drain, and hull 2 cups strawberries. Place 1 cup berries in pan and cover with ½ cup sugar. Add another layer of berries and ½ cup sugar. Cover and let stand at room temperature overnight. Uncover and bring to boil over direct heat. Simmer 15 min., stirring occasionally. Pour into bowl or jar. Cover and let stand at room temperature 24 hr. Store in refrigerator. *Makes 2 cups.*

STRAWBERRY-LEMON PUNCH

A cool and colorful punch to serve for any summer festive occasion.

1½ cups fresh strawberries
½ cup sugar
3 cans (6 oz. each) frozen
   lemonade concentrate
1 qt. ginger ale
ice

Crush berries, add sugar, and let stand ½ hr. Dilute lemonade according to directions on can. Pour into punch bowl. Add strawberries. Just before serving, add ginger ale and ice. *Makes 1½ gal., about 32 servings.*

PRALINE STRAWBERRY SHORTCAKE

1½ cups unsifted Gold Medal
   Flour
3 tsp. baking powder
½ tsp. salt
¼ tsp. soda
½ cup brown sugar (packed)
⅓ cup shortening
½ cup coarsely chopped pecans
1 egg
¾ cup milk
1 qt. strawberries, sweetened

Heat oven to 375° (quick mod.). Grease a round layer pan, 8 x 1½″. Mix first four ingredients. Cut in brown sugar and shortening. Add pecans. Combine egg and milk and stir into flour mixture only until blended. Spread in prepared pan. Bake 20 to 25 min., or until toothpick stuck into center comes out clean. Split into 2 layers. Fill and top with sweetened strawberries. Garnish with whipped cream. *6 to 8 servings.*

1927—First airplane flight completed between California and Hawaii.

1906—Pure Food and Drug Act passed by Congress.

Loud is the summer's busy song,
The smallest breeze can find a tongue,
While insects of each tiny size
Grow teasing with their melodies.
—JOHN CLARE

Flower: Larkspur or Water Lily   **Gem:** Turquoise

Now the heat quivers over fields of ripening grain and bare-foot children skip along the sunburnt grass. The local newspaper sends a reporter out into the noonday heat to fry an egg on the blistering pavement at the corner of State and Main. July, the month honoring Julius Caesar, is the warmest month of the year in most parts of our vast country.

Fruits, vegetables, lean meats, and salads are favorite hot-weather foods. And all of these dishes can be made more interesting with "just a touch" of fresh herbs (see page 73)—so much tastier than the dried ones, and so much fun to grow. Sow herbs as early in spring as weather permits. All they call for is sun and well-drained sandy loam. Only a small space is needed, and the requirements are easily met.

Rule 1: Start small—a few herbs can be as much fun as a gardenful.

Rule 2: Give your plot definition—a friend of mine used a white-painted ladder, placed it level with the soil, and filled each ladder space with a different herb. A spoked wagon wheel would be another attractive idea.

Rule 3: Dig deeply; apply sand for drainage, then fill with soil. Start with chives, thyme, tarragon (perennials), and parsley (a biennial). Fill with annuals sown from seed, such as basil, sweet marjoram, and savory. Use the tall herbs, mint and dill, for accents. I became so fond of my own summer herb garden that I decided to carry it through the long winter months—on a smaller scale, of course—in the flowerbox on my kitchen window sill.

Independence Day, our great national holiday, always seems to be the turning point of summer, an extra excursion day for a special family spree. Mother packs a picnic lunch, and Father digs bait for a day of fishing. Or mindful of long, hot ribbons of cars on crowded concrete highways, the family may decide to have fun at home. This calls for another bag of charcoal for the barbecue, a laundry tub full of ice for cooling drinks, and stretching the badminton net across a shady strip of grass. If you do not already have a lawn game for the yard, investigate lawn bowls, a shuffleboard for the driveway, or a croquet set.

When Planning a Picnic...

Be sure to keep this St. Swithin's Day rhyme in mind:

St. Swithin's Day if it doth rain
For forty days it will remain.
St. Swithin's Day if it be fair
For forty days 'twill rain nae mair.

JULY RED-LETTER FOODS:
GREENS AND BERRIES

Plentiful Vegetables

Beans (Green and Lima)
Beets
Cabbage
Carrots
Cauliflower
Celery
Corn
Eggplant
Greens
Mushrooms
Onions (Green)
Peas
Peppers
Potatoes (New)
Rutabaga
Summer Squashes
Tomatoes
Turnips

Plentiful Fruits

Apricots
Bananas
Blueberries
Cherries
Grapes (Seedless)
Limes
Melons (especially Watermelon)
Oranges (Valencia)
Peaches
Pears (Summer)
Pineapples
Plums
Raspberries
Rhubarb
Strawberries

ABUNDANT GREENS FOR SUMMER

When cooked, 1 lb. serves 3.
For salads, 1 head or 1 lb. serves 4 to 6.

Types of Lettuce:

Iceberg: Most popular; fringed, green leaves — inside leaves more pale.

Cos or Romaine: Cylindrical shape; stiff, coarse leaves—dark green on outside, lighter inside; sweet.

Leaf: Does not form head; loose, curled leaves — light or dark green; crisp.

Bibb: Gourmets' favorite; smooth dark leaves in loose head.

Other Greens:

Beet Tops: Use young ones.

Endive: Curly or French. Curly has ragged, curling, twisted leaves; French is elongated.

Escarole: Like endive, but broader, thicker leaves.

Kale: Cabbage family. Curly leaves; dark leaves best.

Spinach: Large, crisp leaves, either flat or crinkled.

Swiss Chard: Leaf much like spinach, with white midrib.

Water Cress: Tiny leaves.

1

Celebrate summer with fresh blueberry pancakes.

2

"Clouds from south and east may spoil the picnic feast."—Weather Saying

3

"A thing is better for being shared."—English Proverb

4

Independence Day, Declaration of Independence signed in 1776.

5

Cook escarole in consomme and serve the soup with crispy French bread.

6

1928—First "all-talking" motion picture premiered in New York.

7

"Spread the table and contention will cease."—Old Hebrew Proverb

BERRY LUSCIOUS

*Try this to keep the family happy,
the cook and kitchen cool.*

1 cup fine vanilla wafer crumbs
3 tbsp. confectioners' sugar
1/4 cup butter, melted
2 egg whites†
6 tbsp. granulated sugar
1/2 cup whipping cream
1/2 tsp. vanilla
1 pt. fresh raspberries, blackberries, or boysenberries

Mix crumbs, 2 tbsp. of the confectioners' sugar, and butter.
Press into bottom and halfway
up sides of 6 dessert dishes. Chill
until firm. Make meringue by
beating egg whites until frothy
and gradually beating in granulated sugar, a little at a time.
Beat until very stiff and glossy,
about 5 min. Whip cream. Fold
in remaining tbsp. confectioners'
sugar and vanilla. Spoon meringue into prepared dishes.
Sprinkle berries over meringue.
Spread whipped cream over berries. Chill 2 hr. *6 servings.*

Blueberry Luscious: Substitute
1/2 pt. blueberries for raspberries,
blackberries, or boysenberries.

† *See page 172*

❁❁❁❁❁❁❁❁❁❁❁❁❁❁❁

Dinner at
Your Leisure

Braised Pork Chops

Skillet-candied Sweet Potatoes

Buttered Swiss Chard

Radishes and Celery Sticks

*Boysenberry Cobbler

❁❁❁❁❁❁❁❁❁❁❁❁❁❁❁

BOYSENBERRY COBBLER

3 cups fresh boysenberries
3/4 cup water
2/3 to 1 cup sugar
1 tbsp. cornstarch
2 tbsp. cold water
1/4 cup plus 2 tbsp. cream *or*
   1/4 cup milk plus 2 tbsp.
   butter, melted
1 cup Bisquick

Heat oven to 400° (mod. hot).
Heat fruit and water. Stir in
sugar. Dissolve cornstarch in 2
tbsp. cold water and blend into
fruit. Boil 1 min. Pour into 2-qt.
baking dish. Dot with butter;
sprinkle with cinnamon. Mix
cream and Bisquick thoroughly
with fork. Drop dough by spoonfuls onto hot fruit. Bake about
20 min. Serve warm with cream.
6 to 8 servings.

Note: 2 1/2 cups canned boysenberries with juice (1 lb. 4 oz.) may
be substituted for fresh berries
and water; use smaller amount
of sugar.

8

1835—Liberty Bell cracked, tolling the death of Chief Justice Marshall.

9

"Good friends and good fare are always in season."—French Proverb

10

Hamburgers are juicier with ½ cup milk or water per lb. of meat.

11

1789—U. S. Marine Corps was created by act of Congress.

12

100 B.C.—Julius Caesar, for whom this month was named, born.

13

Enhance tomatoes with basil, fresh or dried.

14

1789—Europe's first "Liberty Day," Bastille Day in France.

❀❀❀❀❀❀❀❀❀❀❀❀❀

Quick-to-Fix Lunch

Creamed Tuna on

Crisp Chinese Noodles

*Fresh Spinach Salad

Melon à la mode

❀❀❀❀❀❀❀❀❀❀❀❀❀

FRESH SPINACH SALAD

½ lb. washed fresh spinach,
   finely shredded (3 to 4 cups)
1 small Bermuda onion, minced
¼ cup diced celery
4 hard-cooked eggs, sliced

Toss vegetables and eggs. Chill. Just before serving, toss with French dressing. *6 to 8 servings.*

WILTED GREENS

This salad should be served while the dressing is still hot.

Fry 4 slices bacon, cut up, until crisp. Add ¼ cup vinegar, 2 tbsp. water. Heat. Pour over 1 qt. shredded greens (lettuce, spinach, endive, romaine, or a combination) tossed with 2 green onions, chopped, 1 tsp. salt, and pepper. Sprinkle 1 hard-cooked egg, chopped, on top. *6 servings.*

SKILLET LAMB AND SPINACH

The Far Eastern influence. Unusual, easy, so delicious on rice.

2 cloves garlic, crushed
¼ cup fat or vegetable oil
1 tsp. salt
½ tsp. pepper
½ cup diced onion
2 lb. lean lamb, cut in 1″ strips,
   ¼″ thick
1 cup water
2 lb. fresh spinach
¼ cup soy sauce
¼ cup cornstarch

In large heavy skillet or Dutch oven, sauté garlic in fat 3 min. over low heat, stirring constantly. Remove garlic. Stir salt, pepper, and onion into hot fat in skillet. Add lamb strips; brown over medium heat, stirring constantly. Add ½ cup of the water. Cook, covered, over very low heat until meat is tender (about 1 hr.), adding more water, if necessary. Add spinach. Cook, covered, 3 to 5 min., stirring once or twice. Stir in a mixture of remaining ½ cup water, soy sauce, and cornstarch. Cook, stirring constantly, until thickened. Serve with cooked rice or riced potatoes. *8 to 10 servings.*

15

St. Swithin's Day, honoring the English bishop of the 800's.

16

1945—Atomic Age began with test explosion at Almagordo, N. Mex.

17

"Cloudy skies, smoky haze—warmer nights, cooler days."—Weather Saying

18

"Bagpipes only sing when the belly is full."—Scotch Proverb

19

Sliced ripe olives are a spicy addition to creamed tuna.

20

"Solid pudding is better than empty praise."—English Proverb

21

"Beware of meat twice boiled, and a foe reconciled."—Franklin

EGGS FLORENTINE

Cook 1 lb. fresh spinach just until tender; drain. Season. Chop finely. Heat oven to 400° (mod. hot). Spread spinach in 8" round or square baking dish. Arrange 4 hard-cooked eggs, cut in halves, on top. Cover with 1 cup Medium White Sauce (p. 157). Sprinkle with Crumb Topping (below). Bake 20 min. *4 servings.*

Crumb Topping: Melt 2 tbsp. butter. Add 1 clove garlic, sliced. Cook slowly about 3 min. Remove from heat; remove garlic. Mix in ½ cup dry bread or cracker crumbs and 2 tbsp. grated cheese.

Note: 2 pkg. (10 oz. each) frozen spinach may be used if fresh spinach is not available.

Brunch on the Patio

Broiled Grapefruit Halves

*Eggs Florentine

Sausage Patties

Blueberry Muffins, Butter

To Please the Ladies

Cheese Soufflé with Mushroom Sauce

*Greens in Ramekins

Tomato Halves with Italian Dressing

Melba Toast

*Fruit Parfaits

GREENS IN RAMEKINS

Cut up cooked greens (spinach is delicious) using kitchen shears. Season with butter, salt, pepper, and either crisp bacon bits, nutmeg, or onion. Pack into buttered ramekins (individual molds) or custard cups. Keep warm in very low oven until ready to serve, 15 to 20 min. Unmold and garnish with lemon and hard-cooked egg slices.

FRUIT PARFAITS

Layer fresh, sweet cherry halves or fresh cantaloupe cubes or fresh strawberries, raspberries, or blueberries with vanilla ice cream in parfait glasses, allowing about ¼ cup fruit per serving. Freeze parfaits 15 to 30 min. (if frozen longer than 1 hr., fruit will be icy).

22

"God Almighty first planned a garden."—Francis Bacon

23

"Lettuce is like conversation: it must be fresh and crisp."—Warner

24

"Show me your garden and I shall tell you what you are."—Alfred Austin

25

Circus-time pink lemonade: add grenadine syrup to cold lemonade.

26

1775—Ben Franklin made first postmaster general by Continental Congress.

27

1866—The first trans-Atlantic telegraph cable successfully completed.

28

"After dinner walk a mile, or stand a while."—Roman Health Counsel

Colorful Picnic Salads

KIDNEY BEAN SALAD

2 cups drained cooked kidney
    beans
¼ cup diced celery
3 pickles, chopped (dill or sweet)
1 small onion, minced
2 hard-cooked eggs, sliced
½ tsp. salt
⅛ tsp. pepper
¼ cup mayonnaise or
    commercial sour cream

Mix beans, celery, pickles, onion. Add eggs, seasonings, and mayonnaise, mixing lightly. Chill thoroughly. Garnish with grated cheese.

Chick-Pea or Garbanzo Salad: Make Kidney Bean Salad (above) —except substitute cooked or canned chick-peas or garbanzos for kidney beans.

Ways with Cole Slaw

...for a heartier salad, add a can of tuna or salmon. Use mayonnaise dressing.

...for a lighter salad, add fruit, such as pineapple chunks (drained), sliced bananas, tiny whole green grapes, slices of unpeeled apple.

...mix red and white cabbage for a variety of color.

...salted peanuts add crunch.

Potato Salad Tips

... garnish with anchovies, black olives, cherry tomatoes, hard-cooked egg wedges.

... add cut-up cooked ham, chicken, beef, or veal or canned or frozen lobster or crabmeat for an elegant, hearty luncheon salad.

...for color, add grated carrot and/or chopped pimiento.

GOURMET POTATO SALAD

3 cups cubed cold boiled potatoes
1 tbsp. finely chopped onion
diced whites of 2 hard-cooked
    eggs
½ tsp. salt
dash of pepper
mashed yolks of 2 hard-cooked
    eggs
⅔ cup commercial sour cream
2 tbsp. vinegar
1 tsp. prepared mustard
½ tsp. celery seeds
2 tbsp. mayonnaise
⅓ cup sweet relish

Place potatoes, onion, and egg whites in bowl. Sprinkle with salt and pepper. Mix remaining ingredients; add and toss lightly. *6 servings.*

Quick Potato Salad may be made from Betty Crocker Potato Salad Mix. It also makes wonderful Hot German Potato Salad.

Removing Food Stains

Stain	Method
Chocolate, Cocoa, Coffee with Cream, Cream, Gravy, Ice Cream, Mayonnaise, Meat Juice, Salad Dressing, Sauce, Soup.	Sponge with cool water (washables may be soaked 30 min.). Work in detergent; rinse. If greasy stain remains, sponge with grease solvent, such as carbon tetrachloride.* If colored stain remains, use chlorine or sodium perborate bleach or hydrogen peroxide.
Catsup, Chili Sauce, Eggs, Fruits and Juices, Milk, Soft Drinks, Vegetables.	Sponge with cool water (washables may be soaked 30 min.). If stain remains, work in detergent; rinse. For nonwashables, sponge with alcohol (if safe for fabric**). If stain remains, use chlorine or sodium perborate bleach or hydrogen peroxide.
Wax, Grease, other Greasy Stains.	For washables, work in detergent; rinse or launder. If spot remains, use grease solvent. For nonwashables, sponge with grease solvent. To remove yellow stain on all fabrics, use a chlorine or sodium perborate bleach or hydrogen peroxide.

*Poisonous! Be sure to keep away from eyes and do not breathe in.
**Test at seam or hem.

29

"Eggs and oaths are easily broken."—Proverb

30

1863—Birthday of Henry Ford, pioneer in car manufacturing.

31

"Contentment: getting out of a situation all there is in it."—Chesterton

The sun has drunk
The dew that lay upon the morning grass;
There is no rustling in the lofty elm
That canopies my dwelling, and its shade
Scarce cools me.
—WILLIAM CULLEN BRYANT

Flower: Poppy or Gladiolus   **Gem:** Carnelian or Peridot

August, the month honoring Augustus Caesar, could have been more appropriately christened Month of the Insect Moon. Hot, sultry weather is just what summer pests like. Old pails, tin cans, and containers half-filled with stagnant water are home sweet home for them, especially mosquitoes. Don't encourage them to come and stay. Eliminate their breeding grounds by draining any such containers on or near your patio.

Because of its usually consistent warm weather, August is a good month for vacations. If you have planned to spend this year's vacation on the road, prepare yourself for some helpful backseat driving. Bone up on the historical points along your route—an intelligent guided tour can be fun for all. It's a good idea, too, to make a checklist of emergency supplies that might otherwise be forgotten: raincoats and rubbers; flares and an extra flashlight; tissues, aspirin, bandages, and suntan lotion; and, for Bowser, his water pan, food dish, and blanket.

August heat also calls for special attention to menu planning. How long has it been since you've prefaced a summertime salad or sandwich with a refreshing bowl of chilled soup? Old hot favorites seem to gain a second life when treated this way, especially with an unexpected garnish: cold pea soup with bits of cooked ham or bacon, jellied consommé with thin slices of lemon, cold tomato soup topped with grated cheese or salted whipped cream, consommé "on the rocks" (the hot soup is poured over ice cubes).

Many vegetables are at their best and cheapest this month, so indulge yourself. Cucumber slices or tomato wedges with a liberal sprinkling of salt are perfect sultry-day snacks for jaded appetites. Salt, as you probably know, is especially important during hot weather. Salt insufficiency is one of the prime causes of heat cramps and other less acute afflictions such as dizziness and general fatigue. In addition to a general step-up in the amount of salt used in cooking vegetables, snacks of anchovies and pretzels are pleasant ways to increase your salt intake.

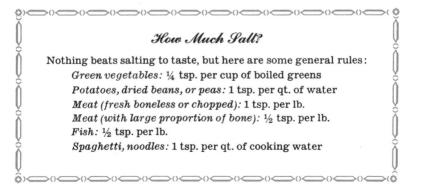

How Much Salt?

Nothing beats salting to taste, but here are some general rules:
> *Green vegetables:* ¼ tsp. per cup of boiled greens
> *Potatoes, dried beans, or peas:* 1 tsp. per qt. of water
> *Meat (fresh boneless or chopped):* 1 tsp. per lb.
> *Meat (with large proportion of bone):* ½ tsp. per lb.
> *Fish:* ½ tsp. per lb.
> *Spaghetti, noodles:* 1 tsp. per qt. of cooking water

```

## AUGUST RED-LETTER FOODS:
## CORN, GREEN BEANS, AND PEACHES

### TIPS ON BUYING CORN
*Buy 1 to 2 ears per person.*

Select ears with green husks and milky kernels growing to tip of ear. Corn is tender if kernel near tip of ear will pierce easily with slight pressure from fingernail.

### PEACH TIPS
*4 medium peaches serve 4.*

Select round, plump, smooth peaches with good color; medium or large size. No blemishes or rot. Avoid soft, cracked peaches. Ripe peaches are very perishable; refrigerate.

| *Plentiful Vegetables* | *Other Available Vegetables* | *Plentiful Fruits* |
|---|---|---|
| Beans (Green and Lima) | Cabbage | Apricots |
| Beets (Early) | Cauliflower | Bananas |
| Carrots | Mushrooms | Blueberries |
| Celery | Peas | Cherries |
| Corn | Rutabagas | Grapes (Concord and Seedless) |
| Cucumbers | Turnips | Limes |
| Eggplant | | Melons (in Variety) |
| Greens | | Oranges (Valencia) |
| Onions (Green and Dry) | | Peaches |
| Peppers | | Pears (Summer) |
| Potatoes | | Plums |
| Summer Squashes | | |
| Tomatoes | | |
```

1

"Dry August and warm doth harvest no harm."—Thomas Tusser

2

"The ripest peach is highest on the tree."—Riley

3

1492—Columbus set sail from Palos, Spain, on his first voyage.

4

"Tart words make no friends."—Poor Richard's Almanac

5

Save watermelon rinds—they will make delicious crisp pickles.

6

1945—The atomic bomb exploded over Hiroshima.

7

"To eat late when hungry is as good as having rich food."—Chinese Proverb

ଦ୍ରୋଦ୍ରୋଦ୍ରୋଦ୍ରୋଦ୍ରୋଦ୍ରୋଦ୍ରୋଦ୍ରୋ

Dad Cooks Out

Barbecued Spareribs
*Grilled Corn
Fresh Fruit Salad
Onion-buttered Hard Rolls
Butter Pecan Ice Cream

ଦ୍ରୋଦ୍ରୋଦ୍ରୋଦ୍ରୋଦ୍ରୋଦ୍ରୋଦ୍ରୋଦ୍ରୋ

GRILLED CORN

Remove large outer husks from young tender ears of corn; turn back inner husks, remove silk. Spread corn with softened butter. Pull husks back over ears, tying with fine wire. Roast on grill over hot coals, turning frequently until done, 20 to 30 min. Serve at once.

FRESH HERB VINEGAR

Lend unique flavor to tossed salads and cole slaw by using herb vinegars in the dressing. Mint vinegar adds tang to fruit punch.

Fill a fruit jar loosely with herbs, such as tarragon, chervil, dill, mint. (Cut the herbs before flowers form; wash and shake thoroughly;dry.) Heat white wine or cider vinegar just to simmering. Pour over herbs. Seal jar and let stand at room temperature for 2 weeks.

HEARTY GREEN BEAN-SAUSAGE CASSEROLE

Tomatoes and green beans add garden-fresh flavor and appealing color to this tempting supper dish.

1 lb. bulk pork sausage
1 cup sliced onion
3 to 4 tbsp. unsifted Gold Medal Flour
2½ cups cooked tomatoes (1 lb. 4-oz. can)
2 cups cooked fresh green beans
½ tsp. salt
½ tsp. pepper
Biscuit Topping (below)

Heat oven to 425° (hot). Brown sausage and onion over low heat. (Break up sausage with fork.) Drain off excess fat. Stir in flour; stir in vegetables and seasonings. Bring to a boil. Pour into 2-qt. baking dish. Immediately top with Biscuit Topping. Bake 20 min. *6 to 8 servings.*

Biscuit Topping: Add ⅓ cup milk all at once to 1 cup Bisquick. Beat hard 20 strokes; knead 8 to 10 times. Roll into 9" circle; cut in 8 wedges.

8

1796—First U.S. passport issued to Mr. Francis Barrere.

9

1779—Francis Scott Key, composer of "The Star Spangled Banner," born.

10

1874—Herbert Hoover, 31st President, born in West Branch, Iowa.

11

If it is not possible to cook corn immediately, keep it refrigerated.

12

1947—The "New Look" exploded upon the fashion world.

13

Lemon juice on peach slices will keep them from darkening.

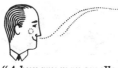

14

"A hungry man smells meat afar off."—Thomas Fuller

๐›๐›๐›๐›๐›๐›๐›๐›๐›๐›๐›๐›

Company-Best Buffet

*Buffet Salmon en Gelée

Parsley-buttered Potatoes

Vegetable Vinaigrette (p. 62)

Pickles and Olives in variety

Tiny Hot Muffins, Butter

Balls of Assorted Fruit Ices

Petits Fours

๐›๐›๐›๐›๐›๐›๐›๐›๐›๐›๐›๐›

BUFFET SALMON EN GELÉE

See picture on pp. 106-107.

6 cups diced celery
2 cups chopped onion
4 lemons, quartered
4 large cloves garlic, minced
12 bay leaves
6 tbsp. salt
2 tbsp. whole allspice
4 tsp. cayenne pepper
6-lb. whole salmon with tail
1½ envelopes unflavored
   gelatin (1½ tbsp.)

First day: Put all ingredients except fish and gelatin in covered pan large enough for fish. (If pan is too small, cut fish in two crosswise.) Add 3 qt. water to seasonings; simmer 15 min.

Wrap fish in cheesecloth, leaving 6 to 8″ ends. Put in pan with stock; cover, simmer 1 hr. (10 min. per lb.). Test meat by thrusting knife into center; meat should be evenly pink throughout. Fish must be thoroughly cooked. Carefully lift fish from pan by grasping ends of cloth. Do not remove cloth as fish is tender. Strain and save 2 cups of stock for glazing. Refrigerate fish.

Second day: Take cloth from fish; peel off skin. With tip of sharp knife, remove gray meat below skin until pink salmon shows evenly on top and sides. Put on large serving platter (fitting two pieces together if salmon is cut in two). Soften gelatin in ⅓ cup strained stock. Heat remaining 1⅔ cups stock to boiling; add gelatin. Take from heat; stir to dissolve. Chill until mixture is the consistency of unbeaten egg whites. Using a pastry brush, generously glaze top and sides of fish (tail, too!) with jellied stock. Chill until set.

Using pimiento, chive sprays, sliced ripe and stuffed olives, yolks and whites of hard-cooked eggs, water cress, and parsley, decorate fish with floral or geometric designs. Soften stock by placing over warm water and stirring. Glaze again to hold design in place. Chill thoroughly. Garnish with leaf lettuce, parsley, and lemon slices. Pass mayonnaise seasoned with fresh dill. *12 servings.*

See page 110 →

Summer

❀❀❀❀❀❀❀❀❀❀❀❀❀❀

Everyone Loves Steak!

Shrimp Cocktail, Salty Crackers

*Steak Continental

*Broiled Zucchini

*Tomatoes Vinaigrette

Hot Dinner Rolls, Butter

Ice Cream with

*Perfection Peach Sauce

❀❀❀❀❀❀❀❀❀❀❀❀❀❀

STEAK CONTINENTAL

Pictured opposite.

2 lb. flank steak or round steak,
   ¾″ thick (cut off all fat)
1 clove garlic, quartered
1 tbsp. salt
2 to 3 tbsp. soy sauce
1 tbsp. tomato paste
1 tbsp. vegetable oil
½ tsp. pepper
½ tsp. oregano leaves

Score both sides of flank steak by cutting ¼″ deep diagonal slices forming diamonds. Mash garlic with salt; add soy sauce, tomato paste, oil, pepper, and oregano. Mix well and rub into steak. Wrap in waxed paper and let stand in refrigerator 5 to 6 hr., or overnight. Broil 5 to 8 min. on each side, or to desired degree of doneness. *4 to 6 servings.*

BROILED ZUCCHINI

Select tender, young, small to medium zucchini squash; cut in half lengthwise. Cook in boiling salted water until just barely tender, about 5 min.; drain very well. Brush with melted butter; sprinkle with salt, pepper, and Parmesan cheese. Broil until butter and cheese brown, 3 to 5 min.

TOMATOES VINAIGRETTE

Marinate tomato halves in Vinaigrette Dressing (p. 62) several hours. Sprinkle with chopped parsley.

PERFECTION PEACH SAUCE

3 fresh peaches, peeled and
   sliced (about 2 cups)
1 tbsp. confectioners' sugar
1 tbsp. lemon juice
¼ cup honey
1½ to 2 tsp. rum flavoring
¼ cup blanched, slivered
   almonds

Rub through a sieve or purée ½ cup peach slices. Sprinkle remaining slices with confectioners' sugar and lemon juice. Combine peach purée, honey, and rum flavoring in saucepan. Bring to boil, stirring occasionally. Stir in remaining sliced peaches with any juice that has accumulated and almonds. Heat through. Serve warm with frozen or refrigerated desserts. *Makes 2 cups.*

FRUIT KABOBS IN A WATERMELON BOAT

Beautiful, showy fruit arrangement that can serve as a glamorous centerpiece. See picture on p. 105.

1 large watermelon
1 qt. fresh strawberries
1½ lb. fresh Bing cherries
1 fresh pineapple *or* 2 cans
    frozen pineapple chunks,
    thawed and drained
1 large cantaloupe
wooden skewers

Cut a very thin slice off the bottom of the watermelon so that it will rest evenly. Cutting horizontally, slice off the top ⅓ of the melon (make melon balls from this piece). With a sharp knife, zigzag the edge of the watermelon boat and remove the fruit to just below the zigzag.

To prepare fruit for kabobs: wash strawberries, leaving stems on. Remove stems from cherries. Cut pineapple into ¾″ chunks. Cut balls from cantaloupe and smaller piece of watermelon. Using wooden or bamboo skewers, assemble kabobs, starting each with a cherry. Stand kabobs in the watermelon boat. This amount of fruit will serve 30 to 35 people, allowing 2 kabobs per person.

PEACHES FLAMBEAU

Plan a party around this exciting dessert.

¼ cup apricot jam
3 tbsp. sugar
½ cup water
4 large fresh peaches *or* 1 can
    (1 lb. 12 oz.) sliced peaches
3 tsp. brandy extract
    (measure at last min.)
¼ tsp. lemon extract
    (measure at last min.)
1 to 2 pt. vanilla ice cream

Have all ingredients and utensils handy on a tray at the table. Simmer jam, sugar, and water in chafing dish until syrupy, 5 to 10 min. Peel and slice fresh peaches or drain canned peaches; add to syrup and cook until almost tender, about 3 min. Just before serving, darken room; combine extracts, pour over peaches, light with a match and let flame until fire is out. Stir to blend flavorings with fruit. Serve over hard ice cream. Garnish with whipped cream and slivered toasted almonds. *4 to 6 servings.*

15

1914—The first ship passed through the Panama Canal: the S.S. Ancon.

16

"Rosemary and rue; keep seeming and savour all winter long."—Shakespeare

17

Cold green beans and cauliflower make an excellent salad.

18

1587—Virginia Dare, first child born to English parents in America.

19

1890—The DAR, Daughters of the American Revolution, organized.

20

"Delay is preferable to error."—Jefferson

21

1859—Oil first struck in the U.S. in Titusville, Pa.

☼)☼)☼)☼)☼)☼)☼)☼)☼)☼)☼)☼)☼)☼)

Supper for a Warm Summer Day

Jellied Consommé, Crisp Crackers

*Green Bean and Egg Salad

Toasted English Muffins

*Peach-Cantaloupe Pie

☼)☼)☼)☼)☼)☼)☼)☼)☼)☼)☼)☼)☼)☼)

GREEN BEAN AND EGG SALAD

1 lb. green beans
6 tbsp. vegetable or olive oil
3 tbsp. vinegar
½ cup minced onion
4 slices crumbled crisp bacon
4 hard-cooked eggs, chopped
3 tbsp. mayonnaise
1 tsp. prepared mustard
2 tsp. vinegar
¼ tsp. salt

Cut beans lengthwise. Cook until tender in 1″ of boiling salted water, about 15 min. Drain and cool. Add oil, 3 tbsp. vinegar, and onion to beans. Salt and pepper to taste. Toss lightly. Chill. Just before serving, stir bacon into beans.

Meanwhile, mix eggs, mayonnaise, mustard, 2 tsp. vinegar, and salt. Heap beans into lettuce-lined bowl. Drop spoonfuls of egg salad over beans. Sprinkle with paprika. *4 to 6 servings.*

PEACH-CANTALOUPE PIE

Pastry for 9″ Two-crust Pie
2 cups fresh peach slices
2 cups thinly sliced cantaloupe
1 cup sugar
¼ cup flour
½ tsp. salt
¼ cup sliced almonds
1 tbsp. butter

Heat oven to 425° (hot). Combine peaches with cantaloupe; toss with mixture of sugar, flour, and salt. Arrange fruit in pastry-lined pie pan. Sprinkle with nuts, dot with butter. Cover with top pastry; bake 35 to 40 min.

Peel Peaches Easily

Dip in simmering water for 30 to 60 seconds, depending on degree of ripeness; then dip into cold water. Slip off the skins.

PEAR SLAW

Crispy cabbage and tangy fruit make a delightfully different salad.

Combine finely chopped cabbage and canned pineapple chunks or tidbits with sweetened mayonnaise for a sweet slaw. On salad plates, arrange a mound of sweet slaw. Core Bartlett pears and cut into 8 thin wedges. Arrange 4 pear wedges on and around each mound of slaw.

22

"Clouds with mushroom tops, bring rain to thirsty crops."—Weather Saying

23

1902—Fannie Farmer opened her cooking school in Boston.

24

1814—British troops captured Washington and burned the Capitol.

25

Sprinkle dill weed lightly over buttered green beans.

26

1920—The 19th amendment, giving women voting rights, went into effect.

27

1914—First jail sentence for auto speeding handed down in Newport, R. I.

28

1922—Station WEAF, New York, broadcast the first paid commercial.

GREEN BEAN SOUP WITH HAM

What aroma could be more mouth-watering than ham simmering in a kettle? Add beans, mmm! Serve with corn bread.

1½-lb. ham bone with meat
7 cups water
8 to 10 whole allspice
6 to 8 sprigs parsley
 (1½ tsp. dried)
2 sprigs summer savory
 (½ tsp. dried)
1 small onion, minced
¼ cup rice
2 cups cut green beans
½ cup sliced carrots

Place ham bone in soup kettle and cover with water. Tie allspice, parsley, and savory in small cheesecloth bag or put in tea ball; drop into kettle. Cover and simmer 2 hr. Add onion, rice, beans, and carrots. Cook 45 to 60 min. more, or until vegetables are tender. Remove spice bag, ham bone, and any excess fat. Pick meat off bone and return to soup. *8 to 10 servings.*

Note: This soup keeps well and is wonderful when reheated.

❁❁❁❁❁❁❁❁❁❁❁❁

Satisfying Sunday Dinner

Broiled Chicken Quarters
Potato Boats with Cheese Sauce
*Polish Beets
Tossed Salad with Tomato Wedges
Whole Wheat Rolls
Fresh Peach Shortcake

❁❁❁❁❁❁❁❁❁❁❁❁

POLISH BEETS

2 tbsp. butter
2 tsp. flour
2 tbsp. vinegar
1 tbsp. sugar
¼ tsp. salt
⅛ tsp. pepper
¼ tsp. dill seeds or dill weed
2 cups freshly cooked beets
 (1 lb.)
Sour Cream Sauce (below)

Melt butter in saucepan. Blend in flour. When bubbly, remove from heat; add vinegar, sugar, salt, pepper, and dill seeds. Stir in beets. Heat through slowly to blend flavors. Serve immediately. Pour warm Sour Cream Sauce over beets. *4 servings.*

Sour Cream Sauce: Blend ½ cup commercial sour cream and 3 to 4 tbsp. cream; warm over low heat.

29

1896—A Chinese chef in New York concocted the first chop suey.

30

"Talkers are no good doers."—Shakespeare

31

"No soup is better than the one you work on."—French Proverb

Popular Salad Dressings

CLEAR FRENCH DRESSING

Mix 1 tbsp. salt, 2 tbsp. sugar, ½ tsp. dry mustard, ¼ tsp. grated onion, ½ tsp. celery seeds, 1 cup vegetable oil, and ½ cup vinegar. Add 1 small peeled clove of garlic. Leave garlic in dressing just 1 hr. Serve with greens.

SOUR CREAM DRESSING

Blend 1 cup commercial sour cream, 1½ tsp. salt, ⅛ tsp. pepper, 3 tbsp. minced chives or onion, 2 tbsp. lemon juice. Delicious with greens or vegetables.

LEMONADE OR LIMEADE DRESSING

Combine ⅓ cup undiluted frozen lemonade or limeade concentrate, ⅓ cup honey, ⅓ cup vegetable oil, and 1 tsp. celery seeds. Beat with rotary beater until blended. Serve with fruit.

RUBY RED DRESSING

Beat ½ cup currant jelly with fork until smooth. Add ¼ cup vegetable oil, 2 tbsp. lemon juice, dash of salt, and few drops onion juice. Beat until smooth with rotary beater. For fruit salads.

The morrow was a bright September morn;
The earth was beautiful as if newborn;
There was that nameless splendor everywhere,
That wild exhilaration in the air,
Which makes the passers in the city streets
Congratulate each other as they meet.
—HENRY WADSWORTH LONGFELLOW

Flower: Aster  **Gem:** Sapphire

It's summer-into-autumn now, with warm days and cool nights and that first golden glow that makes autumn weather so beautiful. It's probably the way the thermometer bobs up and down that gives us that feeling of "wild exhilaration." After Labor Day has come and gone and the children are safely back in school, I always have the urge to do something new— make new friends, join a discussion group, or emote with the local little theater group.

The autumnal equinox, when day and night are of equal length, comes about September 21. From then on, the hours of daylight rapidly diminish and the birds begin to race south with the sun. The little insect-eaters which helped to make your outdoor life last summer more enjoyable, are the first to seek more abundant feeding grounds. A few weeks later, the other birds wing their way south. Some, however, like the chickadee and even some cardinals, stay with you all winter. There are few things more rewarding than spreading the welcome mat for those that remain. Set up a feeding station near your window and watch them during the bleak winter months. Your local Audubon Society or a conservation organization can give you simple suggestions on how to attract our feathered friends.

In the old Roman calendar, September was the seventh month of the year and was called just that—*septima*, the Latin word for seventh. The modern names for October, November, and December were also derived from the original Latin which denoted their positions in the old calendar: *octima*, the eighth month; *novisima*, the ninth month; *decima*, the tenth month.

In many parts of the country late September means the first frost. Whenever a crackling clear evening sky threatens a frost, pick your still-green tomatoes. Cover the biggest ones with newspaper and store them in a warm part of the basement. They'll ripen to perfection. For the smaller ones, discover the joy and satisfaction of home canning. Green tomato pickles are as American as the proverbial apple pie, and anyone would be proud to make it "her specialty." Try your hand, too, at corn relish or watermelon pickles. A repertory of relishes can earn you the compliments of your family and guests. September is pickling and preserving time—and if you've never done it before, now is the time to learn. A shelf filled with jars of jams, chutneys, jellies, and condiments, put up by yourself, is one of the most satisfying accomplishments.

SEPTEMBER RED-LETTER FOODS:
SQUASHES AND MELONS

Plentiful Vegetables	*Other Available Vegetables*	*Plentiful Fruits*
Beans (Green and Lima)	Brussels Sprouts	Apples
Beets (Early)	Corn	Avocados
Cabbage	Greens	Bananas
Carrots	Rutabagas	Grapefruit
Cauliflower	Turnips	Grapes (Tokay and Seedless)
Celery		Lemons
Eggplant		Melons (in Variety)
Onions (Dry)		Oranges (Valencia)
Peppers		Peaches
Potatoes (Mature)		Pears (Summer)
Squashes (Summer and Winter)		Plums
Sweet Potatoes and Yams		
Tomatoes		

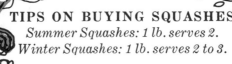

TIPS ON BUYING SQUASHES
Summer Squashes: 1 lb. serves 2.
Winter Squashes: 1 lb. serves 2 to 3.

Summer Squashes (Store in refrigerator.)

White: Cymling, Pattypan, or Scalloped — disc-shaped with scalloped edges; tender.

Yellow: Straight neck or crookneck—lemon color, some warts.

Green: Zucchini — dark green. Chayote and Cocazelle—lighter green.

Winter Squashes (Store in cool, dark, dry place.)

Acorn or Table Queen: Acorn-shaped; hard shell, dark green, ridged.

Butternut: Bell or gourd-shaped; smooth, light-tan skin.

Hubbard: Large, heavy; thick, hard skin with warty surface; orange rind, deep-yellow flesh.

1

"Now if you're ready, Oysters dear, we can begin to feed."—Lewis Carroll

2

1945—Japan surrendered; World War II ended.

3

1609—Henry Hudson discovered the river now bearing his name.

4

"What will a child learn sooner than a song?"—Pope

5

1882—The first Labor Day Parade was held in New York City.

6

1860—Jane Addams, social worker and 1931 Nobel Prize winner, born.

FAVORITE MELONS
Tests for ripeness and descriptions.

Cantaloupe: Ripe if soft near stem end. Coarse netting on green or gray rind. Sweet, fine texture; pungent aroma.

Casaba: Blossom end of melon should be soft. White, juicy meat; firm. Large, round, yellow. Late variety.

Honeydew: Blossom end of melon should be slightly soft. Green, juicy, sweet flesh. Oval; smooth, whitish-green rind.

Persian: Stem end should be soft, with well-defined netting on rind. Large, round melons, resembling cantaloupe. Deep orange-pink flesh, thick and mildly sweet.

Watermelon: Thumps with dull, hollow sound. Should be symmetrical in shape, green color; velvety appearance, yellow underside. Inside is crisp, juicy, red or pink.

MELON FRUIT PLATE

Cool, refreshing, inviting. Serve for brunch, appetizer, or dessert.

Cut ¾" thick cantaloupe slices; remove rind with sharp knife. Arrange melon rings on salad greens and fill center of each ring with fresh fruit. Arrange clusters of Frosted Grapes (below), wedges of fresh pears or peaches, and diagonally cut banana slices around melon ring as desired.

Frosted Grapes: Brush grapes with slightly beaten egg white.†
Dip in granulated sugar. Dry on a rack.

† *See page 172*

7

Fill baked winter squash with a mixture of Lima beans and sour cream.

8

Cantaloupes and peaches are good mates for salads and desserts.

9

1776—Continental Congress made "United States of America" official.

10

1846—The first sewing machine was patented by Elias Howe.

11

1862—Wm. Sidney Porter (O. Henry), master of the short story, born.

12

"Experience is the name everyone gives to his mistakes."—Oscar Wilde

13

Serve melon balls and plum slices on greens with a fruit dressing.

SQUASH WITH SAUSAGE

A favorite for autumn suppers. See picture on p. 141.

Cut acorn squash in half; each half serves one. Heat oven to 375° (quick mod.). Place squash cut-side-down in shallow pan. Bake 20 to 30 min. Turn up; brush with butter; season with salt and pepper. Fill with broken-up bulk sausage. Bake 20 to 30 min., or until squash is tender, sausage brown. Pour off fat before serving.

HONEYED FRUIT PARFAITS

Prepare 6 cups cut-up fruit, combining two in-season fruits: strawberries with cantaloupe balls; green or Tokay grapes with sliced peaches; blackberries with melon balls; or blueberries with peaches. Make Honey Syrup (below). Alternate layers of the two fruits and syrup (2 tbsp. each) in 6 parfait glasses. Garnish with mint. *6 servings.*

Honey Syrup: Boil ½ cup sugar and ¼ cup water 2 to 3 min. Stir in ½ cup honey, ¼ tsp. cinnamon, and ½ tsp. rum extract.

✦✦✦✦✦✦✦✦✦✦✦✦

Get-Together Dinner Party

Veal Paprika

Poppy Seed Noodles

*Corn-Stuffed Zucchini

Fresh Spinach Salad (p. 92)

Hot Rolls

*Honeyed Fruit Parfaits

✦✦✦✦✦✦✦✦✦✦✦✦

CORN-STUFFED ZUCCHINI

6 medium zucchini squash
1 can (12 oz.) whole kernel corn *or* 1½ cups fresh corn
2 tsp. seasoned salt
1 tsp. salt
¼ cup chopped onion
¼ cup chopped chives
½ cup grated Cheddar cheese

Heat oven to 350° (mod.). Cut off zucchini ends; do not pare. Cook whole in boiling water 5 to 7 min. Cut zucchini in half lengthwise. Carefully remove flesh from shells, leaving a ¼" rim; chop. Drain well; squash will be watery. If using fresh corn, cut from ears and cook 5 min. Drain corn well; combine with chopped zucchini, salt, onion, and chives. Place zucchini shells in 13 x 9" baking dish. Pile corn mixture lightly into shells. Sprinkle with cheese. Bake uncovered 30 min. *6 servings.*

14

1778—Benjamin Franklin appointed first U.S. envoy to France.

15

Spoon brown sugar into acorn squash for the last half of baking.

16

1620—The "Mayflower" sailed from Plymouth, England.

17

"Credulity is the man's weakness but the child's strength."—Lamb

18

1793—George Washington laid the cornerstone of the Capitol.

19

When serving summer squash, add a dash of marjoram.

20

"If you love honey fear not the bees."—French Proverb

VEGETABLES AND MEAT BALLS ITALIANO

Superb combination of vegetables, meat, and seasonings. Serve with tossed greens, bread sticks, and spumoni.

Spicy Meat Balls (right)
1 medium onion, thinly sliced
½ cup chopped celery
2 tbsp. butter
1 can (6 oz.) tomato paste
1½ cups water
1 envelope (1½ oz.) dry
  spaghetti sauce mix
4 zucchini squash
1 small eggplant
1 medium green pepper
3 medium tomatoes
½ cup vegetable oil
½ tsp. dry basil
¼ lb. Mozzarella cheese, grated
1 pkg. (8 oz.) noodles

Make Spicy Meat Balls. Meanwhile, sauté onion and celery in butter in 1½-qt. saucepan. Add tomato paste, water, and spaghetti sauce mix; simmer slowly about 5 min.

Cut unpeeled squash in ¼″ crosswise slices. Peel eggplant; slice thinly and cut each slice into quarters; cut green pepper into 1″ cubes; cut tomatoes into small wedges. In Dutch oven or large kettle, sauté vegetables in hot oil until limp, 15 to 20 min. Add hot spaghetti sauce, basil, most of cheese, and Spicy Meat Balls. Cook over low heat 15 to 20 min. Cook noodles according to directions on pkg.; drain and butter. Serve noodles topped with vegetable-meat ball mixture and sprinkled with cheese. *8 servings.*

For a flavorful, meatless main dish, omit meat balls.

Spicy Meat Balls: Mix ingredients for Piquant Meat Loaf (p. 150). Shape into balls the size of large walnuts (about 30). Brown on all sides in hot fat. Cover and cook 30 min.

21

"Wear a good hat; the secret of your looks."—Oliver Wendell Holmes

22

"The scarlet of the maples can shake me like a cry."—Carman

23

Try different breads for lunch box variety.

24

"A gourmet would rather go hungry than eat good food in haste."—Reyniere

25

"Heap high the farmer's wintry hoard! Heap high the golden corn."—Whittier

26

1820—Daniel Boone died in Charette, Montana.

27

Tomato relish is a delicious accompaniment to meats.

GREEN TOMATO-APPLE RELISH

3 large green tomatoes
3 large tart apples
3 small onions
1¼ cups vinegar
1¼ cups sugar
¾ tsp. ginger
¼ tsp. turmeric
¼ tsp. salt

Remove blossom ends from tomatoes; pare apples and cut away the cores; peel onions. Work tomatoes, apples, and onions through a food grinder, making certain to catch all the liquid. Transfer ground mixture to a large strainer and drain off ½ cup of the liquid. Discard this amount. Combine ground mixture with remaining liquid. Heat vinegar, sugar, ginger, turmeric, and salt in 2-qt. saucepan. Cook until liquid boils vigorously; remove from heat and add the ground tomato mixture. Bring back to boil, reduce heat and simmer 5 min. Spoon hot relish into sterilized pint jars and seal. *Makes 2 to 3 pints.*

WATERMELON PICKLES

6 cups water
9 cups pared watermelon rind, cut into ¾″ squares (for color, leave a thin layer of red pulp on rind)
4 cups sugar
1 cup white vinegar
¼ tsp. oil of cinnamon
¼ tsp. oil of cloves

First day: Bring water to boil in large saucepan. Add watermelon rind and simmer until rind is tender when pierced with fork, 10 to 15 min. Drain thoroughly and place in glass bowl. Combine sugar, vinegar, oils of cinnamon and cloves in saucepan; bring to boil, stirring until sugar is dissolved. Pour syrup over rind. Cool; cover and let stand overnight.

Second day: Drain rind, reserving syrup. Heat syrup to boil; pour over rind. Cool; cover and let stand overnight.

Third day: Repeat as directed for second day.

Fourth day: Heat rind and syrup to boil. If desired, add 1 or 2 drops red or green food coloring. Immediately pack pickles in sterilized jars and seal tightly. *Makes about 3 pints.*

ISABEL'S FRESH PEAR CHUTNEY

5 lb. firm ripe Bartlett pears (about 20 medium)
½ cup finely chopped green peppers
1½ cups seedless raisins
4 cups sugar
1 cup chopped candied ginger
3 cups cider vinegar
½ tsp. *each* salt, cloves, and allspice
3 sticks whole cinnamon

Pare, core, and slice pears lengthwise into ¼″ slices. Combine with green peppers, raisins, sugar, ginger, vinegar, and salt in 6-qt. saucepan. Tie cloves, allspice, and cinnamon in cheesecloth bag. Add to mixture in saucepan. Simmer uncovered until dark and syrupy, about 3 hr. Remove spice bag. Spoon into hot sterilized jars and seal at once. *Makes about 4 pints.*

OLD-FASHIONED TOMATO PRESERVES

4 qt. yellow plum or red cherry tomatoes*
¼ cup water
sugar
2 lemons, juice and slivered rind
½ cup finely cut-up candied ginger

Cut tomatoes in quarters. Place in large heavy saucepan or kettle. Add water and bring to boil; boil 10 min. Measure boiled tomatoes; measure an equal amount of sugar and add to tomatoes. Add lemon juice, small slivers of lemon rind, and ginger. Simmer 3 to 3½ hr., stirring occasionally. Preserves thicken as they cool. Pour into sterilized jars; seal with paraffin. *Makes about 6 pints.*

*Larger tomatoes may be substituted. Cut in small pieces before measuring. Omit water.

"Art may err, but Nature cannot miss."—Dryden

28

"Stubble Geese at Michaelmas are seen upon the spit."—King

29

Scoop out baked squash and mash with cream and nutmeg.

30

His store of nuts and acorns now
The squirrel hastes to gain,
And sets his house in order for
The winter's dreary reign.
—JOYCE CARY

Flower: Calendula or Cosmos   **Gem:** Opal or Tourmaline

October always reminds me of the frisky squirrel that makes his winter home somewhere in the vicinity of my backyard. As I do my dishes, I can watch him as he buries a hickory nut in the ground, just at the edge of the dogwood clump. He rapidly scoops out a small hole with both paws and stealthily drops in the nut, turning his head this way and that lest some improvident acquaintance discover his cache. Then, balancing on his hind legs, he pats the ground smooth with a fine show of satisfaction. After he has arranged a small twig over the buried nut, as a masterful touch, he flicks a fallen leaf, ever so casually, to one side of his treasure trove.

October temperatures correspond to those for April, but, of course, in reverse. Killing frosts may be expected as far south as western Maryland and southern Minnesota by the first of the month, and in southern North Carolina and south-central Oklahoma by the end. This, then, is the time to plant next spring's bulbs, the ones that give your garden the most spectacular early display. Place them close together in clumps in a sunny sheltered spot for earliest bloom. Small crocuses bloom earlier than their larger cousins, as will snowdrops, one of the first harbingers of spring. The beginning of September through mid-December is bulb-planting time almost everywhere except in warm climates. There, bulbs should be planted later, any time through January.

Don't forget the leaves that come twirling down from the trees. They should be raked off the grass and piled into your shrubbery border to serve as mulch. Or carry them to your compost pile. There your leaves will become one of nature's finest plant foods.

October brings us "Indian summer," the name given to that mild, dry, hazy weather which follows the first frost. In England this seasonal phenomenon is called "goose summer," for it was at that time that the geese, which had been fattened, were eaten. Spiders weave furiously during "goose summer"; that is probably why anything very sheer reminds us of the bedewed "gossamer" webs which cross our paths these October mornings.

"From ghoullies and ghosties and long-leggety beasties and things that go bump in the night, good Lord deliver us!" What would October be without Halloween, that night of trick and treat, when the children dress up and roam from house to house. Let the grown-ups get in on the fun, too, with an old-fashioned Halloween party—bobbing for apples, biting doughnuts off strings, and all the other old favorites. You'd be surprised how much fun you can have.

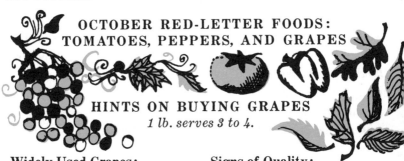

OCTOBER RED-LETTER FOODS: TOMATOES, PEPPERS, AND GRAPES

HINTS ON BUYING GRAPES
1 lb. serves 3 to 4.

Widely Used Grapes:

Concord: Eastern grape; blue-black; medium, slip-skin; compact clusters.

Thompson Seedless: Western grape; greenish-white; always seedless; medium, thin skins; tender, firm.

Tokay or Flame Tokay: Western grape; large, red, oval; has seeds; thick skins.

Signs of Quality:

Buy mature, plump grapes, firmly attached to stems; high color for variety. Not moldy, wet, or shriveled.

Buy for Purpose:

Use all three types mentioned in salads or for table use; Concord grapes are especially good for juice or jelly.

Plentiful Vegetables	*Other Available Vegetables*	*Plentiful Fruits*
Beans (Green and Lima)	Artichokes	Apples
Beets (Late)	Broccoli	Avocados
Cabbage	Brussels Sprouts	Coconuts
Carrots	Cauliflower	Cranberries
Celery	Celery Root	Grapefruit
Cucumbers	Greens	Grapes
Eggplant	Mushrooms	Melons (Casaba
Onions (Dry)	Rutabagas	and Persian)
Peppers	Turnips	Oranges
Potatoes (Mature)		(Valencia)
Sweet Potatoes and Yams		
Tomatoes		
Turnips		
Winter Squashes		

1

"There is something in October, sets the Gypsy blood astir."—Carman

▲▲▲

2

"Eaten bread is soon forgotten."—Welsh Proverb

▲▲▲

3

1873—Emily Post, the authority on etiquette and manners, born.

▲▲▲

4

"A Fireside is a great opiate "—Leigh Hunt

▲▲▲

5

Mix brown sugar and sour cream; serve over seedless green grapes.

▲▲▲

6

1880—The Mormons in Utah renounced polygamy.

▲▲▲

7

"Wrinkles disfigure a woman less than ill nature."—Dupuy

◊)◊)◊)◊)◊)◊)◊)◊)◊)◊)◊)◊)

Dine in Elegance

*Brittany Duck

*Rice Casserole

Cauliflower garnished with bacon bits

Buttered Broccoli

Rolls

Grape Cheese Pie (p. 140)

◊)◊)◊)◊)◊)◊)◊)◊)◊)◊)◊)◊)

RICE CASSEROLE

1 cup raw white rice
1 can chicken broth
½ can water
1 medium onion, chopped
¼ cup butter
1 can (6 oz.) mushrooms,
    drained
½ tsp. salt

Heat oven to 350° (mod.). Place all ingredients in a 1½-qt. baking dish. Cover. Bake 1 hr. Stir occasionally. Garnish with chopped parsley or chives. *6 servings.*

BRITTANY DUCK

5 to 6-lb. duck, quartered
⅓ cup unsifted Gold Medal
    Flour
2 tbsp. shortening
1 onion, finely chopped
1 clove garlic, minced
3 tbsp. chopped parsley
1 tbsp. paprika
1 bay leaf
1 tsp. salt
¼ tsp. pepper
¼ tsp. thyme
1 cup apple cider

Heat oven to 350° (mod.). Wash and dry meat; dredge in flour. Brown duck in hot shortening in heavy skillet, 10 to 15 min. on each side. Remove excess fat as it accumulates. Meanwhile chop giblets finely and cube liver. Remove duck from skillet, drain and arrange in 13 x 9½ x 2″ pan or Dutch oven. Sprinkle chopped giblets, cubed liver, and seasonings over duck, pouring on cider last. Cover; bake 1½ to 2 hr., or until tender. *4 to 6 servings.*

Brittany Chicken: Use a 5 to 6-lb. roasting chicken, cut up, in place of duck; bake 1¼ to 1½ hr.

8

1871—Mrs. O'Leary's cow started the Great Chicago Fire.

▲▲

9

" 'Tis not the meat but the appetite makes eating a delight."—Suckling

▲▲

10

1900—Helen Hayes, First Lady of the American theatre, born in Baltimore.

▲▲

11

Run hot boiled shrimp under cold water to ease the peeling job.

▲▲

12

Columbus Day—a legal holiday in most states.

▲▲

13

1792—Cornerstone of White House laid.

▲▲

14

✥⟩❂⟩✥⟩❂⟩✥⟩❂⟩✥⟩❂⟩✥⟩❂⟩✥⟩

Old Country Flavor

Fall Fruit Cup
*Hungarian Stuffed Peppers
Spinach and Lettuce Salad
Bread Sticks
Gingerbread with Whipped Cream

✥⟩❂⟩✥⟩❂⟩✥⟩❂⟩✥⟩❂⟩✥⟩❂⟩✥⟩

FAR EAST EGGPLANT

Try this with broiled hamburgers and lettuce wedges for an easy supper.

¼ cup olive or vegetable oil
1 clove garlic, minced
1 green pepper, chopped
1 onion, chopped
1 medium eggplant, cubed
4 tomatoes, cut up
2 tsp. salt
¼ tsp. pepper
2 tbsp. grated Parmesan cheese
6 slices crisp crumbled bacon

Cook ingredients except cheese and bacon in skillet until tender. Top with cheese and bacon. Brown under broiler. *4 servings.*

HUNGARIAN STUFFED PEPPERS

8 medium green peppers
½ lb. ground beef
½ lb. ground lean pork
1 cup cooked rice (½ cup uncooked)
1 slice bread, cubed
2 tsp. salt
1 small clove garlic, mashed
2 cans (8 oz. each) tomato sauce
1 tbsp. sugar
1½ tsp. salt
1 tsp. lemon juice

Cut tops from peppers; remove seeds and membranes. Cook in boiling water 5 min. Drain. Mix ground meats, rice, bread cubes, salt, and garlic thoroughly. Fill peppers with mixture. Set in saucepan just large enough to permit peppers to stand upright. Mix remaining ingredients. Pour over peppers. Cover pan tightly and simmer 1 hr. to 1 hr. 15 min. Remove peppers from pan with spatula; drain off liquid and pour over peppers. *8 servings.*

15

"No man can lose what he never had."—*Izaak Walton*

16

Grapes, melon balls, and diced apples make a good fall fruit cup.

17

1758—Noah Webster, father of the American dictionary, born.

18

"Let Ignorance talk as it will, learning has its value."—*La Fontaine*

19

1814—"The Star Spangled Banner" was sung for the first time, in Baltimore.

20

"Every sweet has its sour, every evil its good."—*Emerson*

21

Sauté tomato halves in butter; serve with cream browned in same skillet.

BROILED SANDWICH DE LUXE

Perfect after-the-game snack, served with potato chips and crisp relishes.

Heat oven to 450° (hot). Make Biscuit Dough (below). Spread on greased baking sheet to make oblong, 10 x 8″. Spread with soft butter. Bake 10 to 12 min. Meanwhile, slice 1 large tomato into 8 slices; season. Spread 8 slices of boiled ham with prepared mustard. Cut 8 slices of cheese large enough to cover tomato and ham. Cut baked biscuit into 8 squares. Top with tomato, ham, and cheese. Broil until cheese melts. Serve immediately. *8 servings.*

Biscuit Dough: Add ⅔ cup milk all at once to 2 cups Bisquick. Beat hard 20 strokes.

Variations: Use 1 can (6½ oz.) tuna moistened with mayonnaise, cooked bacon strips, or slices of turkey or chicken in place of ham and mustard.

BEEF-TOMATO NOODLE SOUP

Homey, spicy, so thick it's almost a stew, so satisfying it's a meal in itself.

3 medium onions, chopped
3 tbsp. butter
2 lb. round steak, cut in 1″ cubes,
   or 2 lb. beef stew meat
2 tsp. salt
⅛ tsp. pepper
2 tsp. paprika
2 cans (6 oz. each) tomato paste
2 cans (10½ oz. each) consommé
4 cups water
2 medium green peppers,
   coarsely diced
4 oz. (½ pkg.) noodles
3 cloves garlic, minced
½ tsp. caraway seeds
⅓ cup finely chopped parsley
¼ tsp. marjoram

Sauté onions in butter until golden; add beef, salt, pepper, and paprika. Cook covered over low heat 15 min. Add tomato paste, consommé, and water. Cook covered until meat is nearly done, 1½ to 2 hr. Add green pepper and cook uncovered 30 min. longer. Meanwhile, cook noodles until tender. Drain noodles and add to soup last 10 min. of cooking. A few minutes before serving, add remaining seasonings. Serve in soup bowls with French bread. *8 to 10 servings.*

22

1833—The Metropolitan Opera opened with a performance of "Faust."

23

"The night shows stars and women in a better light."—Byron

24

1901—Anna Edson Taylor went over Niagara Falls in a barrel and survived.

25

Sauté sliced eggplant, tomatoes, and green pepper together for a treat.

26

"Your friend is one who knows you and still likes you."—Hubbard

27

Theodore Roosevelt, Rough Rider and 25th president, born.

28

Raw green pepper strips or rings add color to a relish tray.

◊⟩◊⟩◊⟩◊⟩◊⟩◊⟩◊⟩◊⟩◊⟩◊⟩◊⟩

Halloween Party for Grown-ups

*Pumpkin Chiffon Tarts

Salted Nuts

Hot Spiced Punch   Coffee

◊⟩◊⟩◊⟩◊⟩◊⟩◊⟩◊⟩◊⟩◊⟩◊⟩◊⟩

PUMPKIN CHIFFON TARTS

8 Baked Tart Shells
1 envelope unflavored gelatin
    (1 oz.)
⅔ cup brown sugar (packed)
½ tsp. salt
½ tsp. *each* cinnamon, nutmeg,
    and ginger
1¼ cups cooked or canned
    pumpkin
3 egg yolks
½ cup milk
3 egg whites
½ cup sugar†
¼ tsp. cream of tartar

Blend gelatin, sugar, seasonings, pumpkin, egg yolks, and milk in saucepan. Cook over medium heat, stirring constantly, just until it boils. Remove from heat. Chill until mixture mounds slightly when dropped from a spoon. Make meringue of egg whites, sugar, and cream of tartar; fold into pumpkin mixture. Pour into cooled tart shells. Chill 2 hr., until set. Garnish with whipped cream. *8 tarts.*

† *See page 172*

OLD-FASHIONED OATMEAL COOKIES

Spicy-good! For trick-or-treaters, for after-school snacks, or for a schoolroom party. See picture on pp. 142-143.

1 cup seedless raisins
1 cup water
¾ cup soft shortening
1½ cups sugar
2 eggs
1 tsp. vanilla
2½ cups unsifted Gold Medal
    Flour
½ tsp. *each* baking powder and
    cloves
1 tsp. *each* soda, salt, and
    cinnamon
2 cups rolled oats
½ cup chopped nuts

Simmer raisins and water slowly until plump, 20 to 30 min. Drain liquid into measuring cup. Add water to make ½ cup. Heat oven to 400° (mod. hot). Cream shortening, sugar, eggs, and vanilla; stir in raisin liquid. Stir flour, leavenings, and seasonings together; blend in. Add oats, raisins, and nuts. Drop rounded teaspoonfuls about 2″ apart on ungreased baking sheet. Bake 8 to 10 min., or until browned. *Makes 7 doz.*

29

1929—Panic on Wall Street, the start of the depression.

▲▲

30

"Sin has many tools, but a lie is the handle which fits all of them."—Holmes

▲▲

31

"Bless this house from ... the nightmare and the goblin."—Cartwright

Planting Chart for Spring-Flowering Bulbs

September 1 to December 15 is planting time for most spring-flowering bulbs—about 4 weeks before the ground freezes is a good rule of thumb. In warm climates, however, bulbs should be planted later—anytime through January.

The following bulbs are grouped according to their approximate blooming times.

	Depth	Spacing		Depth	Spacing
Very Early:			*Early to Mid-Season:*		
Crocus crysanthus	3"	3"			
Glory-of-the-Snow (Chinodoxa)	3"	3"	Daffodils (short cup)	4"	5"
Snowdrop (Galanthus)	3"	3"	Daffodils (other species)	6"	6"
Winter Aconite (Eranthis)	3"	3"	Dogtooth Violet	3"	3"
Early:			Guinea Hen Flower (Fritillaria)	4"	8"
			Hyacinth	4"	6"
Grape Hyacinth (Muscari)	3"	2"	Tulips (small)	4"	5"
Siberian Squill	3"	3"	*Mid-Season to Late:*		
Spring Snowflake	4"	4"	Wood Hyacinth	3"	3"
			Tulips	6"	6"

◊⫯◊⫯◊⫯◊⫯◊⫯◊⫯◊⫯◊⫯◊⫯◊⫯◊⫯◊⫯

When Friends Come

Breaded Veal Cutlet

Sweet Potatoes

Beets in Orange Sauce

Celery, Olives, and Turnip Sticks

Onion Buns

*Grape Cheese Pie

◊⫯◊⫯◊⫯◊⫯◊⫯◊⫯◊⫯◊⫯◊⫯◊⫯◊⫯◊⫯

GREEN GRAPE PIE

9" Baked Pie Shell
¾ cup sugar
3 tbsp. cornstarch
1 qt. seedless green grapes
   (stems removed)
¼ cup water
1 tbsp. lemon juice
1 cup commercial sour cream
1 tbsp. sugar
1 tsp. vanilla

Combine sugar and cornstarch in saucepan. Add grapes and water. Cook over low heat about 5 min., stirring constantly, until thickened. Remove from heat; stir in lemon juice. Chill thoroughly. Pour into cooled pie shell. Mix cream, sugar, and vanilla; spread evenly over top. Chill 2 to 3 hr. Serve garnished with whole or halved fresh green grapes.

GRAPE CHEESE PIE

See picture on pp. 142-143.

8 or 9" Baked Pie Shell
1 pkg. (8 oz.) cream cheese
1 envelope unflavored gelatin
   (1 tbsp.)
⅓ cup sugar
¼ tsp. salt
¾ cup orange juice
1 egg, separated
1 tbsp. lemon juice
1 tbsp. sugar
1 cup halved seeded Tokay
   grapes or halved green grapes
½ cup whipping cream, whipped

Let cream cheese come to room temperature. In small mixer bowl, whip cream cheese until fluffy on high speed. Blend gelatin, sugar, and salt in heavy saucepan; add orange juice and slightly beaten egg yolk. Cook over medium heat, stirring constantly, until mixture comes to a boil; boil 1 min. Add to cream cheese while beating on low speed on mixer. Add lemon juice. Chill until mixture mounds when dropped from spoon.

Beat egg white in small mixer bowl until frothy; gradually add 1 tbsp. sugar and continue beating until stiff; fold into cream cheese mixture. Fold in grapes and whipped cream. Spoon into cooled baked pie shell. Chill until firm, about 2 hr. Garnish with whipped cream and additional halved, seeded grapes. *6 to 8 servings.*

See page 122 →

Fall

See page 164

See page 138

See page 12

See page 140

See page 152

☼)☀)☼)☀)☼)☀)☼)☀)☼)☀)☼)☀)☼)

Western Get-Together

*Burgers and Spaghetti,
Barbecue Style
Raw Vegetable Relishes
Crisp Bread Sticks
Devils Food Cake

☼)☀)☼)☀)☼)☀)☼)☀)☼)☀)☼)☀)☼)

WESTERN BARBECUE SAUCE

2 tbsp. fat
½ cup chopped onion
1 clove garlic, minced
1 can (7 oz.) mushrooms, sliced
mushroom liquid and water to
    make ½ cup
3 cans (8 oz. each) tomato sauce
1 cup diced green pepper
    (1 medium)
½ tsp. dry mustard
2 tbsp. brown sugar
1 tsp. chili powder
1 tsp. barbecue spice
¾ tsp. salt
¼ tsp. pepper
dash of Tabasco
½ cup grated Cheddar cheese

Sauté onion, garlic, and mushrooms in hot fat until onion is transparent. Add rest of ingredients—except grated cheese—and simmer 20 min. Stir in cheese until melted. May be made ahead and refrigerated.

BURGERS AND SPAGHETTI, BARBECUE STYLE

Pictured opposite.

Western Barbecue Sauce (left)
1½ lb. ground beef
1½ tsp. salt
¼ tsp. pepper
¾ cup water
½ cup chopped onion
12 to 16 oz. spaghetti
6 green peppers

Prepare Barbecue Sauce. Make hamburgers: toss ground beef, salt, pepper, water, and onion together lightly with fork; divide and form into 6 thick patties. Handle as little as possible. Arrange patties on cold broiler pan or on outdoor grill. Brush patties with Barbecue Sauce. Broil 3″ from heat, turning once. Brush again with sauce. Do not flatten. Allow 5 to 8 min. cooking per side. While hamburgers are broiling, cook spaghetti and green peppers.

Wash green peppers and slit in half lengthwise. Remove seeds, stems, and ribs. Cook in boiling water 4 to 5 min., until just fork tender.

Cook spaghetti following manufacturers' directions. Pile immediately into cooked pepper shells.

Serve both spaghetti-stuffed peppers and broiled hamburgers with Barbecue Sauce. *6 servings.*

We thank thee then, O Father,
For all things bright and good,
The seed-time and the harvest,
Our life, our health, our food.
—19TH CENTURY HYMN

Flower: Chrysanthemum   **Gem:** Topaz

When we turn the calendar to November, our thoughts rapidly fly to the end of the month and Thanksgiving, that wonderful family day of fine food and equally fine conversation.

The first Thanksgiving by presidential proclamation was celebrated on November 26, 1789; following that, no regular holiday was set aside for many decades. But thanks to the untiring efforts of one woman, we now have our annual national day of Thanksgiving. Sarah Josepha Hale, editor of the famous *Godey's Lady's Book*, started her campaign in the 1830's, stressing the idea that "Thanksgiving, like the Fourth of July, should be a national festival observed by all our people." It was not until 1863, however, that her campaign succeeded, when President Abraham Lincoln proclaimed the last Thursday in November as Thanksgiving Day. Now it is always the fourth Thursday in November.

Thanksgiving makes most of us think of turkey, the conventional fare for the day. Everyone loves this fowl, so be sure there's enough to go around and around...and maybe around again. Allow ½ to ¾ pound of the ready-to-cook weight per serving. And to some the stuffing is as important to the Thanksgiving feast as the noble bird itself. Stuffings vary from region to region, from family to family—in Baltimore, oyster stuffing is the favorite; while in the South, corn bread predominates. The basic ingredient may be bread, corn bread, or rice—made tastier with oysters or mushrooms; chestnuts, walnuts, or pecans; sausage meat, liver, or veal; or fruits such as dried apricots. All provide flavor and texture. To moisten a too-dry stuffing, use butter or margarine, meat broth or consommé, cider, or fruit juices. And don't forget spices and herbs!

A Newlywed's First Dinner Party

Soup
Fish
A Boiled Ham
A Boiled Turkey with Oyster Sauce
Three Roasted Ducks and Dish of Scalloped Oysters
Potatoes, Turnips, Parsnips, Celery
Pudding, Pastry, Fruit
Coffee

The above menu, recommended for a young, inexperienced housekeeper, was taken from a leaf of Miss Beecher's *Domestic Receipt Book,* published in 1848. Remember it when you feel overwhelmed by the culinary demands of Thanksgiving dinner.

NOVEMBER RED-LETTER FOODS:
POTATOES AND APPLES

Plentiful Vegetables	*Other Available Vegetables*	*Plentiful Fruits*
Cabbage	Artichokes	Apples
Carrots	Beets (Late)	Avocados
Cauliflower	Broccoli	Cranberries
Celery	Brussels Sprouts	Grapefruit
Eggplant	Celery Root	Grapes (Tokay
Peppers	Greens	and Concord)
Potatoes	Mushrooms	
Sweet Potatoes	Onions (Dry)	
and Yams	Rutabagas	
Tomatoes		
Turnips		
Winter Squashes		

TIPS ON BUYING APPLES
3 medium apples equal 1 lb. or 3 cups, sliced.
Use 2 to 2½ lb. for pie.

Apples for General Use:

Baldwin, Jonathan, King David, McIntosh, Northern Spy, Wealthy, Winesap.

Apples for the Fruit Bowl:

Delicious, Golden Delicious, Red Delicious, Gravenstein, Grimes Golden, Winesap.

Apples for Cooking or Baking:

Baldwin, Greening, Rome Beauty, Winesap, Jonathan, Duchess, Wealthy.

Signs of Quality:

Firm, with good color. No shriveling of peel. Immature fruit lacks color and flavor.

Storage:

Store in cool, dry place, or in refrigerator.

1

"Chill November's surly blast made fields and forests bare."—Scott

2

Dip a lettuce leaf in soup to skim fat quickly.

3

"Virtue is like a rich stone—best plain set."—Bacon

4

1940—FDR was the first President elected to a third term.

5

Try dill leaves instead of parsley on boiled potatoes.

6

1901—Kate Greenaway, famous illustrator of children's books, died.

7

1805—Marie Curie, discoverer of radium, born.

◖◗◖◗◖◗◖◗◖◗◖◗◖◗◖◗◖◗◖◗

Supper
from the Oven

*Piquant Meat Loaf

*Baked Potato Cream

Buttered Green Peas

*Apple-Cabbage Salad

Caraway Rolls

Chocolate Fudge Cake

◖◗◖◗◖◗◖◗◖◗◖◗◖◗◖◗◖◗◖◗

PIQUANT MEAT LOAF

3 medium slices soft bread, torn
   in small pieces, *or* 1 cup dry
   bread crumbs
1 cup milk (1¼ cups for dry
   crumbs)
1 lb. ground beef
½ lb. ground lean pork
½ cup minced onion
1 egg, slighty beaten
¼ cup prepared mustard
1 can (4 oz.) pimiento, diced
1 tbsp. paprika
2 tsp. salt
1 tsp. oregano leaves
½ tsp. black pepper

Heat oven to 350° (mod.). Combine bread and milk. Add remaining ingredients and mix well. Pat
mixture into greased loaf pan,
9 x 5 x 3″. Bake 1½ hr. *8 servings.*

BAKED POTATO CREAM

6 cups raw diced potatoes
1 cup cream (20% butterfat)
1 tsp. salt
⅛ tsp. pepper
2 tbsp. butter
2 tbsp. dry bread crumbs

Heat oven to 350° (mod.). Place
potatoes in buttered 1½-qt. baking dish. Pour cream and seasonings over potatoes. Dot with butter; sprinkle top with bread
crumbs. Bake uncovered 1¼ to
1½ hr., or until potatoes are fork
tender. *6 servings.*

APPLE-CABBAGE SALAD

1½ cups finely shredded
   cabbage
1 tart apple, cut in julienne
   strips (about 1 cup)
1 tbsp. finely minced onion
   or chives
1 tbsp. vinegar
2 oz. crumbled Roquefort or
   Bleu cheese
¼ cup commercial sour cream
   thinned with 1 to 2 tbsp.
   light cream *or* ½ cup
   whipping cream, whipped

Toss cabbage, apple strips (reserving a few for garnish), onion,
and vinegar. Crumble in cheese.
Toss with cream. Dip reserved apple in lemon juice; garnish top of
salad. Chill. *4 to 6 servings.*

8

1837—Mount Holyoke Women's College opened.

9

"Unbidden guests are often welcomest when they are gone."—Shakespeare

10

Before using, crush dried herbs in palm with fingertips.

11

Veterans' Day, replacing Armistice Day.

12

Two to four-day-old bread is best for stuffing.

13

1921—Audiences swooned at first showing of "The Sheik" with Valentino.

14

1832—Horse-drawn street cars made first appearance in New York City.

✧◈✧◈✧◈✧◈✧◈✧◈✧◈✧

For the Men

*Beef Steak Pie
Green Beans with Pimiento
Rye Bread
*Crusty Baked Apples

✧◈✧◈✧◈✧◈✧◈✧◈✧◈✧

BEEF STEAK PIE

1 lb. round steak, cut into 1"
  cubes
3 small onions, thinly sliced
3 tbsp. flour
1½ tsp. salt
¼ tsp. pepper
dash *each* thyme and garlic salt
2 cups water
3 medium potatoes, pared and
  thinly sliced

Heat oven to 350° (mod.).
Dredge meat in flour. Brown in
skillet in 3 tbsp. fat until very
brown, about 15 min. per side.
Add onions and cook until golden
brown, about 10 min. Put in 2-qt.
baking dish. Sprinkle with flour,
salt, pepper, thyme, and garlic
salt; pour water over top. Bake
45 min. to 1 hr. Remove from
oven; increase oven temperature
to 425° (hot). Place potatoes on
top and sprinkle with salt and
paprika. Bake about 30 min. longer, until potatoes are tender. *4 to
6 servings.*

CRUSTY BAKED APPLES

See picture on pp. 142-143.

2 cups unsifted Gold Medal Flour
1 tsp. salt
¾ cup lard (add 2 tbsp. if using
  hydrogenated shortening)
¼ cup water
6 medium apples, pared and
  cored

Heat oven to 425° (hot). Mix
flour and salt. Cut in lard. Sprinkle with water; mix with fork.
Round into ball. Divide into 6
parts. Roll each part into an 8"
round on lightly floured board.
Place apple in center of each
round; fold pastry over apple.
Place on baking sheet, sealed-
side-down. Cut slits in top. Brush
with milk and sprinkle with sugar. Bake 35 min. Serve warm
with Fluffy Sauce. *6 servings.*

Fluffy Sauce: Beat ½ cup soft
butter, 1 cup sifted confectioners'
sugar, 1 egg, and 1 tsp. vanilla
together with electric mixer or
rotary beater.

15

"The best mirror is an old friend."—Herbert

16

"He that is giddy thinks the world turns 'round."—Shakespeare

17

Serve baked apples with a ruffle of whipped cream.

18

1883—Standard Time was adopted throughout the U. S.

19

1863—Lincoln's Gettysburg address.

20

1620—Peregrine White, first white child in New England, born.

21

1922—Rebecca Felton, first woman to hold U. S. Senate office, appointed.

Christmas cooky baking can be started in late November. Seal fruity cookies and keep in a cool place. Most baked cookies and cooky doughs can be frozen.

HOLIDAY SPRITZ

1 cup soft butter
⅔ cup sugar
3 egg yolks
1 tsp. rum flavoring
2½ cups unsifted Gold Medal
   Flour

Heat oven to 400° (mod. hot). Mix well butter, sugar, egg yolks, flavoring. Work flour in with hands. Tint dough with food coloring to light pastel shades. Force dough through cooky press onto ungreased baking sheet in "S" shapes, rosettes, fluted bars, or other desired shapes. Bake 7 to 10 min., until set but not brown. Glaze cooled cookies with Butter Rum Glaze. *Makes about 6 doz.*

Butter Rum Glaze: Melt ¼ cup butter in saucepan. Blend in 1 cup sifted confectioners' sugar and 1 tsp. rum flavoring. Stir in 1 to 2 tbsp. hot water until glaze spreads smoothly. Tint glaze to match cookies.

JEWELED BROWNIE CAKES

Heat oven to 350° (mod.). Make Cake-like Brownies as directed on Betty Crocker Brownie Mix pkg. —except add 2 cups chopped candied fruit to batter. Pour into 15 medium paper-lined muffin cups, filling to top. Bake 25 min. Serve warm with Hard Sauce. *15 servings.*

Hard Sauce: Cream until soft ½ cup butter (¼ lb.); gradually blend in 1 cup sifted confectioners' sugar. Beat in 1 unbeaten egg white; stir in ½ tsp. vanilla. Put in serving dish; sprinkle with nutmeg; chill about 1 hr.

MINCEMEAT DATE BARS

Heat oven to 400° (mod. hot). Using 1 pkg. Betty Crocker Date Bar Mix, combine crumbly mixture and date filling mix with 1 egg, ¼ cup hot water, ½ cup chopped nuts, and 1 cup mincemeat. Spread in greased oblong pan, 13 x 9½ x 2". Bake 20 to 25 min. Frost while warm with Thin Icing. Cut into bars. *Makes 4 doz.*

Thin Icing: Blend 1½ cups sifted confectioners' sugar, 3 tbsp. cream, ½ tsp. vanilla, and ½ tsp. almond flavoring.

22

"Keep your eyes open before marriage, half shut afterwards."—Franklin

23

"What calls back the past, like the rich pumpkin pie?"—Whittier

24

1869—American Woman Suffrage Association held first meeting in Cleveland.

25

"Lost Time is never found again."—Franklin

26

1789—First official Thanksgiving Day celebration in the U. S.

27

A pinch of curry powder lends an Oriental touch to creamed turkey.

28

1942—Coffee rationing began in World War II.

ᐤᑕᐤᑕᐤᑕᐤᑕᐤᑕᐤᑕᐤᑕᐤᑕᐤᑕᐤ

Thanksgiving Dinner

Hot Spiced Apple Juice

Vegetable Relishes
with Sour Cream Dip

Roast Turkey, Sage Dressing

Mashed Potatoes, Turkey Gravy

Cranberry Ice (p. 162)

Carrots au Gratin (p. 52)

Broccoli with Lemon Butter

Perfection Salad

Crescent Rolls

*Fruits of the Harvest Cake

ᐤᑕᐤᑕᐤᑕᐤᑕᐤᑕᐤᑕᐤᑕᐤᑕᐤᑕᐤ

*Give no more to every guest
Than he's able to digest:
Give him always of the prime;
And give but little at a time;
Give to all but just enough,
Let them neither starve nor
stuff,
And that each may have
his due,
Let your neighbour carve
for you.*
—SIR WALTER SCOTT

FRUITS OF THE HARVEST CAKE

Try your hand at cake decorating.

Bake and frost cake: Bake Betty Crocker Honey Spice Cake Mix. Fill and frost with 1 pkg. Betty Crocker Caramel Fudge Frosting Mix.

Make fondant: Mix 1 pkg. Betty Crocker Creamy White Frosting Mix, ½ cup soft butter, and ½ tsp. almond flavoring with fork. Work with hands to form a ball. Knead 20 to 30 times on board lightly dusted with confectioners' sugar.

Shape decorations: Reserve ¼ cup fondant and tint remainder with orange food coloring. Using 1 tbsp. each, shape 18 tiny pumpkins of orange fondant, making ridges around pumpkin sides with toothpick. Tint 2 tbsp. reserved fondant green; shape into tiny squashes. Tint 2 tbsp. reserved fondant red; shape into tiny apples. Arrange these miniature fruits of the harvest on and around the frosted cake.

TURKEY SANDWICH EN CASSEROLE

Delicious from the golden, toasty top to the creamy, meaty bottom.

Place warmed leftover turkey (sliced breast or diced meat) in a shallow greased baking dish. Pour hot Cheese Sauce (below) over top. Cover with triangular bread slices. Broil until browned, about 5 min.

CHEESE SAUCE

To 1 cup Medium White Sauce (right) add ¼ tsp. dry mustard with the seasonings. Blend in ½ cup nippy Cheddar cheese (cut up or grated). Stir until cheese is melted.

MEDIUM WHITE SAUCE

2 tbsp. butter
2 tbsp. flour
¼ tsp. salt
⅛ tsp. pepper
1 cup milk

Melt butter over low heat in a heavy saucepan. Blend in flour and seasonings. Cook over low heat, stirring until mixture is smooth and bubbly. Remove from heat. Stir in milk. Bring to boil, stirring constantly. Boil 1 min. *Makes 1 cup.*

29

1832—Louisa May Alcott, author of "Little Women," born.

30

1835—Samuel Clemens, whose pen name was "Mark Twain," born.

DECEMBER

Now Christmas comes,'tis fit that we
Should feast and sing and merry be,
Keep open house, let fiddlers play
A fig for Cold, sing care away....
—VIRGINIA ALMANACK, 1766

Flower: Holly   **Gem:** Turquoise

December is a month of happy anticipation, of rustling tissue paper, telltale bits of tinsel, mixing bowls of butter-rich dough, and the punch bowl lifted from its hiding place by careful hands. December means caroling and Christmas morning, New Year's Eve and *Auld Lang Syne*. December means nostalgia, too, with memories of yuletides past and of once-loved toys spied under Christmas tree branches of long ago.

The Christmas tree has a long and fascinating history. A thousand years ago, in Germany, the fir tree was hung with apples to depict the Garden of Eden in Christmas miracle plays. In later years, it was brought into the house and decorated with cookies shaped like angels, dolls, and stars. As time passed, trees became prettier and prettier. Legend has it that one of the first real Christmas trees in America was that of the homesick Hessian soldiers in Trenton in 1776, who passed the time decorating it while General Washington crossed the Delaware.

Candles, the yule log, and mistletoe are beloved symbols of Christmastime. The lighted candle has had religious significance for centuries, going back to the Old Testament and the ancient Hebrew Festival of Lights. From England, where it was introduced by the Vikings, comes the yule log, generous enough in size to burn from Christmas Eve to the Feast of the Epiphany, and around which everyone gathered to sing carols. The custom of kissing under the mistletoe comes down to us from ancient Druid rites. Mistletoe was believed to have magical healing and fertility powers, and kissing beneath it portended happiness, health, and good luck.

First-footing is an amusing custom of the British Isles, particularly Scotland. On New Year's Eve, the visitor whose foot is first to cross the threshold after midnight decides his host's luck for the coming year. Dark-haired men are luckier than blond ones, while red-haired men and women of any complexion are bad luck. A first-footer must never come empty handed, for something must be brought into the house before anything can be taken out—or bad luck will strike.

Wrapping gifts is such fun! Why not suggest to some of your friends that they bundle their unwrapped gifts and wrapping materials into the clothes basket and come over to your house to work at one end of the dining-room table while you do up your gifts at the other? Coffee and a delicious cake afterwards will make it a truly festive occasion. Or organize a progressive present-wrapping party with some other good friends and go from house to house. Whatever you do, bring a bit of old-fashioned warmth into our modern streamlined yuletide.

DECEMBER RED-LETTER FOODS:
CAULIFLOWER, CRANBERRIES, AND AVOCADOS

Plentiful Vegetables	*Other Available Vegetables*	*Plentiful Fruits*
Broccoli	Artichokes	Apples
Cabbage	Brussels Sprouts	Avocados
Carrots	Celery Root	Cranberries
Cauliflower	Eggplant	Grapefruit
Celery	Greens	Lemons
Potatoes (Mature)	Mushrooms	Oranges (Navel)
Sweet Potatoes	Onions (Dry)	Pears (Winter)
and Yams	Parsnips	
Turnips	Peppers	
Winter Squashes	Rutabagas	

TIPS ON BUYING AVOCADOS
Buy individually. Sizes vary from 6 to 12 oz.

Signs of Quality:

Softness to slight pressure indicates ripeness. Thin-skinned varieties have better flavor; light markings that resemble scabs do not affect flesh. Unripened fruit may be ripened at room temperature in 4 to 5 days. Avoid overripe or soft fruit and breaks in skin.

Store Carefully:

Ripe avocados are very perishable; should be refrigerated. To prevent darkening of cut fruit, dip in lemon or grapefruit juice, vegetable oil, or sprinkle with a powdered ascorbic acid preparation.

1

In the tropics, avocado is spooned into hot soup.

~~~~~~

2

1816—First Savings Bank opened in Philadelphia.

~~~~~~

3

"That best of fame—a rival's praise."—Moore

~~~~~~

4

"If you keep a thing seven years, you are sure to find a use for it."—Scott

~~~~~~

5

Creamy cauliflower-potato soup is a warming winter dish.

~~~~~~

6

St. Nicholas' Day, a European feast day.

~~~~~~

7

1787—Delaware became the first state to ratify the Constitution.

❁❁❁❁❁❁❁❁❁❁❁❁❁❁❁❁

December Ladies' Luncheon

Cheese Soufflé

with Creamed Chicken or Turkey

Crisp Rye Rounds

Balls of *Cranberry Ice

and Pistachio Ice Cream

❁❁❁❁❁❁❁❁❁❁❁❁❁❁❁❁

CRANBERRY ICE

1 qt. cranberries (4 cups)
2 cups water
2 cups sugar
¼ cup lemon juice (2 lemons)
1 tsp. grated orange rind *or*
    ½ cup orange juice
2 cups cold water

Cook cranberries in water until skins are broken, about 10 min. Rub through a fine sieve to make smooth pulp. Stir in rest of ingredients. Pour into refrigerator tray. Freeze until firm, 2 to 3 hr., stirring 2 or 3 times. *8 servings.* Serve in avocado halves as an appetizer, in small scoops as an accompaniment to roast turkey, or as a dessert.

CRANBERRY DELIGHT PIE

Perfect for any holiday party.

8″ Baked Pie Shell
½ lb. marshmallows
½ cup milk
¾ cup ground fresh cranberries
    (2 to 2½ cups unground)
1 tbsp. grated orange rind
1 cup whipping cream, whipped

Place marshmallows and milk in top of double boiler; heat over hot water until marshmallows melt. Then chill until the consistency of thick whipped cream. Drain excess juice off cranberries until quite dry. Fold in cranberries and orange rind. Chill until thick (almost holds shape when spatula is drawn through). Fold in whipped cream. Pour into cooled pie shell. Chill until set (about 2 hr.). Remove from refrigerator 20 min. before serving.

Cranberries Are Here

• Cranberries should be cooked only until they pop open.
• For a different fresh cranberry sauce, cook them in orange juice instead of water.
• If you want to keep cranberries as fresh as the day you bought them, put them packaged as they are into your freezer. They will keep for months.

8

1886—American Federation of Labor founded.

~~~~~~

9

"You are what you think and not what you think you are."—Hubbard

~~~~~~

10

1820—Emily Dickinson, America's first great poetess, born.

~~~~~~

11

"Jealousy is the jaundice of the soul."—Dryden

~~~~~~

12

Top a slice of jellied cranberries with Waldorf salad and whipped cream.

~~~~~~

13

"He that complies against his will, is of his own opinion still."—Butler

~~~~~~

14

1799—George Washington died at Mount Vernon.

CAULIFLOWER AND TOMATOES PARMESAN

Cauliflower cooked Italian-style. Good with ham, green rice, and salad.

1 medium cauliflower
1 tsp. salt
1 tsp. lemon juice, if desired
1 small clove garlic, minced or
    crushed
2 tbsp. olive or vegetable oil
½ tsp. salt
1 large fresh tomato, cut into
    8 to 10 wedges
1 tsp. chopped parsley
2 tbsp. grated Parmesan or
    Cheddar cheese

Wash cauliflower; separate into medium cauliflowerets. Place in pan; barely cover with water. Add 1 tsp. salt and lemon juice (to keep cauliflower white). Cover; boil 10 min., or until just barely tender. Drain. In large skillet sauté garlic in oil until browned. Add cauliflowerets and sauté lightly. Add ½ tsp. salt and tomato wedges; cover and simmer 2 to 3 min., or until tomatoes are softened slightly. Serve sprinkled with parsley and cheese. *4 to 5 servings.*

Note: 1 pkg. (10 oz.) frozen cauliflower and 1 large canned tomato, drained, may be substituted for fresh vegetables.

◊⟩◊⟩◊⟩◊⟩◊⟩◊⟩◊⟩◊⟩◊⟩◊⟩◊⟩◊⟩

Holiday Week Coffee Klatsch

Fingers of Red Apples and

Winter Pears in bowl of ice

Hot Cinnamon Streusel Coffee Cake

*Cranberry-Orange Nut Bread

*Cocoa-flavored Coffee

◊⟩◊⟩◊⟩◊⟩◊⟩◊⟩◊⟩◊⟩◊⟩◊⟩◊⟩◊⟩

CRANBERRY-ORANGE NUT BREAD

See picture on p. 142.

¾ cup sugar
1 egg
1¼ cups orange juice
1 tbsp. orange rind
3 cups Bisquick
¾ cup chopped nuts
1 cup chopped fresh cranberries

Heat oven to 350° (mod.). Mix sugar, egg, orange juice, rind, and Bisquick. Beat vigorously 30 seconds. Batter may still be lumpy. Stir in nuts and cranberries. Pour into well-greased loaf pan, 9 x 5 x 3″. Bake 55 to 60 min., until toothpick stuck into center comes out clean. Crack in top is typical. Remove from pan. Cool before slicing.

COCOA-FLAVORED COFFEE

Stir 1 tbsp. cocoa into 6 cups freshly brewed hot black coffee.

15

Sprinkle grated cheese on cauliflower and broil until cheese melts.

16

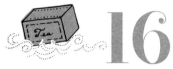

1773—Boston Tea Party; colonists protested against the tea tax.

17

1903—First successful flight by the Wright brothers at Kitty Hawk, N. C.

18

"Dare to be true: nothing can need a lie."—Herbert

19

Glaze baked pears with maple syrup.

20

1820—Missouri levied the first "Bachelor Tax" in the U. S.

21

The first day of winter.

✿⟩✿⟩✿⟩✿⟩✿⟩✿⟩✿⟩✿⟩✿⟩✿⟩✿⟩✿⟩

Christmas Day Dinner

Hot Tomato Cocktail

*Piquant Dip with Crackers or Chips

Prime Ribs of Beef au Jus

Potato Puff

Cauliflower with Cheese Sauce

Peas and Carrots with Mushrooms

*Avocado-Citrus Salad

Traditional Christmas Breads

Steamed Plum Pudding

with Hard Sauce (p. 154)

✿⟩✿⟩✿⟩✿⟩✿⟩✿⟩✿⟩✿⟩✿⟩✿⟩✿⟩✿⟩

PIQUANT DIP

½ cup cottage cheese
1 cup commercial sour cream
1 hard-cooked egg, finely
    chopped
¼ cup minced green pepper
1 tbsp. catsup
1½ tsp. prepared horse-radish
1 tsp. Worcestershire sauce
½ small clove garlic, minced
½ tsp. dry mustard
½ tsp. salt

Mix cottage cheese and sour cream thoroughly. Stir in remaining ingredients. Cover and chill 2 hr. to blend flavors. Serve as a dip for crackers, potato chips, or vegetable relishes. *Makes 1½ cups.*

AVOCADO-CITRUS SALAD

An easy-to-make salad combining fruits that are plentiful during the winter.

Halve avocado crosswise and remove seed. Peel each half and slice into ¼″ rings. Sprinkle with lemon juice (to keep avocado from darkening) and salt. Arrange 3 rings on plate of water cress or parsley. Place 1 or 2 segments of orange or grapefruit on each ring. Pass Lemonade Dressing (p. 115).

AUNTIE'S DATE-APPLE PUDDING

A butterscotchy pudding rich in apples, dates, and nuts.

1 cup brown sugar (packed)
¼ cup cornstarch
2¼ cups water
1 cup chopped dates
1 cup chopped apples
2 tbsp. butter
¼ tsp. vanilla
1 cup broken walnuts

Mix brown sugar and cornstarch in 2-qt. saucepan. Gradually stir in water. Cook over medium heat, stirring constantly, until mixture boils; boil 1 min. Add dates, apples, butter, and vanilla. Remove from heat. Cool to room temperature, add nuts, then chill. Serve in sherbet glasses. Top with whipped cream, if desired. *6 to 8 servings.*

22

"Ring 'round the moon—snow before noon."—Weather Saying

23

Christmas cauliflower: serve with strips of pimiento and green pepper.

24

" 'God bless us everyone!' said Tiny Tim, the last of all."—Dickens

25

MERRY CHRISTMAS!

26

Today's the day to start writing those thank-you notes.

27

"They that govern most make the least noise."—Selden

28

1869—Chewing gum patented by W. F. Semple.

✿❀✿❀✿❀✿❀✿❀✿❀✿❀✿❀

New Year's Eve Supper

Roast Capon with Pecan Stuffing

Cream Gravy

Mint-glazed Carrots

Cranberry-Orange Relish

Crescent Rolls

*Rose Petal Ice Cream

Tiny Butter Cookies

Coffee

Mints

✿❀✿❀✿❀✿❀✿❀✿❀✿❀✿❀

ROSE PETAL ICE CREAM

1 qt. vanilla ice cream
1/4 tsp. nutmeg
1 tbsp. rose water (available in
  drugstores)

Let ice cream soften slightly;
stir in nutmeg and rose water.
Refreeze. Before serving, arrange
scoopfuls of rose petal ice cream
on platter decorated with rose-
buds and leaves.

Holiday Punch Bowl

Cut a sturdy circle of styrofoam to fit around the base of
the bowl. Poke small holes in
the styrofoam and insert festive greens or flowers. When
using flowers, wrap stems in
wet cotton first.

NEW YEAR'S EVE PUNCH

*As a change from the traditional
eggnog, you can make this refreshing punch which will cer-
tainly please your family and
guests.*

1 can (6 oz.) frozen concentrated
  grapefruit juice
1 can (6 oz.) frozen concentrated
  lemonade
1 can (6 oz.) frozen concentrated
  orange juice
1 qt. apple cider, chilled
1 pkg. (10 oz.) frozen
  strawberries, thawed and
  drained
1 qt. ginger ale, chilled

Add 1 1/2 cups water to grapefruit juice; mix well; pour into
ice cube tray. Add 1 1/2 cups water
to lemonade; mix well; pour into
ice cube tray. Freeze.

Chill punch bowl. Dilute orange
juice with 3 cans water. Pour into
punch bowl; add cider, 2 cups water, and strawberries. Thirty minutes before serving, add fruit
cubes; allow to thaw, thus adding
flavor to punch. Ten minutes before serving, add ginger ale.
Makes 3 1/2 qt.

1851—YMCA organized in Boston.

"Never love unless you can bear with all the faults of man."—Campion

"Eating pork at midnight brings good luck."—New Year's Eve Saying

"Just Too Pretty to Open!"

• A sleigh of gifts: sleigh runners of stiff silver matte paper, gaily decorated and pasted along the sides of a stack of wrapped packages.

• A Christmas surprise for a child: a gift package growing a border of French flower-faced lollipops.

• A package of spiced, sugared nutmeats adorned with a cluster of gilded walnuts.

• A gift bearing a sugar cooky Christmas tree ornament: beautifully frosted and embellished, the cooky is held in place and kept edible by a double wrap of saran about the package.

• Extra-special jam or jelly: triple-wrap the jar with red, pink, and green tissue paper; draw ends together and perk into a big pouf on top. The final touch —a sprig of mistletoe.

Table of Food Equivalents

FOOD	WEIGHT	APPROXIMATE MEASURE
Apples	1 lb.	3 medium (3 cups sliced)
Bananas	1 lb.	3 medium (2½ cups sliced)
Berries	1 qt.	3½ cups
Bread crumbs, fresh	1-lb. loaf	8 cups fresh bread crumbs
Butter, margarine, lard, or shortening	1 oz.	2 tbsp.
	1 stick (¼ lb.)	½ cup
	1 lb.	2 cups
Candied fruit	½ lb.	1½ cups
Cheese, Cheddar or American	¼ lb.	1 cup grated
Cheese, cream	3-oz. pkg.	6 tbsp.
Cheese, cottage	12-oz. carton	1½ cups
Coffee, ground	1 lb.	80 tbsp. (enough to make 40 cups of coffee)
Chocolate, unsweetened	½-lb. pkg.	8 1-oz. squares
Cocoa	4 oz.	1 cup
Coconut, shredded	1 lb.	5 cups
Cream, whipping	½ pt.	1 cup (2 cups whipped)
Cream, sour	12-oz. carton	1½ cups
Dates, pitted	7¼-oz. pkg.	1¼ cups, cut up
Egg whites	4	½ cup
Egg yolks	6	½ cup
Flour		
All-purpose	1 lb.	3½ cups unsifted
Cake	1 lb.	4 cups unsifted
Whole wheat	1 lb.	3½ cups unsifted

FOOD	WEIGHT	APPROXIMATE MEASURE
Lemon	1 medium	1½ to 3 tsp. grated rind and 2 to 3 tbsp. juice
Macaroni	7 or 8-oz. pkg.	4 cups cooked
Marshmallows	¼ lb.	16
Milk		
Evaporated	6-oz. can	¾ cup
	14½-oz. can	1⅔ cups
Sweetened condensed	15½-oz. can	1½ cups
Noodles	5 or 6-oz. pkg.	2½ cups cooked
Nuts, in shell		
Almonds	1 lb.	1 to 1¾ cups nutmeats
Peanuts	1 lb.	2¼ cups nutmeats
Pecans	1 lb.	2¼ cups nutmeats
Walnuts	1 lb.	1⅔ cups nutmeats
Nuts, shelled		
Almonds	1 lb.	3½ cups nutmeats
Peanuts	1 lb.	3 cups nutmeats
Pecans	1 lb.	4 cups nutmeats
Walnuts	1 lb.	4 cups nutmeats
Oranges	1 medium	1 to 2 tbsp. grated rind and ⅓ to ½ cup juice
Potatoes, sweet	1 lb.	3 medium (3 cups sliced)
Potatoes, white	1 lb.	3 medium (2⅓ cups sliced)
Raisins	15-oz. pkg.	3 cups
Rice, white	1 cup	3 to 4 cups cooked
Rice, wild	1 cup	3 cups cooked
Spaghetti	7 or 8-oz pkg.	4 cups cooked
Sugar		
Granulated	1 lb.	2 cups
Brown	1 lb.	2¼ cups (packed)
Confectioners'	1 lb.	3½ cups (sifted)

TODAY'S FOOD SAFETY

Food safety concerns have changed over the years. We no longer can enjoy recipes using raw eggs that aren't cooked or baked. However, today we can substitute pasteurized eggs and safely enjoy these recipes. You can find cartons of pasteurized eggs in the refrigerator section of the grocery store. Or use a pasteurized fat-free cholesterol-free egg product. It is available in cartons in the refrigerator or freezer section of your grocery store.

Please use only pasteurized eggs in the following recipes. Remember, it will take up to twice as long to beat pasteurized egg whites to form stiff peaks.

Broccoli with Broiled Mayonnaise (page 10)
Orange Baked Alaskas (page 14)
3-Egg White Meringue (page 14)
Banana Chiffon Pie (page 22)
Crème Vanille Heart (page 24)
Lemon Schaum Torte (page 32)
Rhubarb Ice Cream (page 64)
Berry Luscious (page 90)
Frosted Grapes (page 120)
Pumpkin Chiffon Tarts (page 138)

RECINE INDEX